HE HAD TO BREAK ME TO BLESS ME

My Journey of Restoration

ASHLEY MAGEE MADRY

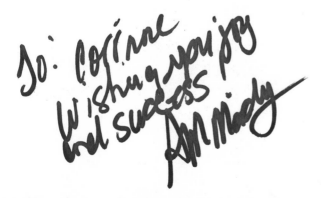

To: Corinne
Wishing you joy
and success
AMMadry

ISBN 978-1-64258-457-8 (paperback)
ISBN 978-1-64258-458-5 (digital)

Christian Faith Publishing, Inc.
832 Park Avenue
Meadville, PA 16335
www.christianfaithpublishing.com

Scripture quotations taken from the 21st Century King James Version®, copyright © 1994. Used by permission of Deuel Enterprises, Inc., Gary, SD 57237. All rights reserved.

Printed in the United States of America

DEDICATION

This book is dedicated to my parents, the late Ernest and Annie Magee. I am thankful for the love and Christian guidance they provided me for twenty-two years. Without their love and guidance, I would not be the person I am today. I am most thankful for my mom introducing me to Jesus Christ.

CONTENTS

AUTHOR'S NOTE

This is an inspirational work of nonfiction. It's based on true experiences I have encountered in my life and my interpretation of those experiences. Each experience impacted my journey of restoration and spiritual growth and maturity. Throughout this work, I referenced Scriptures from the King James Version of the Bible. The interpretation of Scriptures are based on my understanding and study of the word of God. I pray this work will inspire you on your life's journey.

ACKNOWLEDGMENTS

I thank God for bringing me through the most difficult times of my life and giving me the courage to share those times with others. I sincerely thank my sister Robin Magee Cox for allowing me to share our tragedies with others. I am also thankful for her support and consultation throughout this process. Thanks to my husband Shane and our two children Sydni and Caleb for their love, encouragement, and belief in me. Special thanks to my pastors Jerry and Felicia Brown for their Biblical guidance and belief in my ability to minister to others through my writing. Their ministry was influential in writing this book and continues to assist in my spiritual growth. Thank you to my Lifeline Church family and all the family and friends that provided words of encouragement and support throughout this journey.

PREFACE

We are living in a world and a time of great uncertainty. Few things in life are known and certain, but as years have passed, even things we thought were known and certain have become uncertain. Believers and nonbelievers are losing hope, lacking faith, and questioning God. As a Christian, I was inspired to write this book to be transparent and be able to share my personal struggle for understanding and peace following traumatic experiences in my life. Often, Christians are afraid and reluctant to be transparent when their belief and faith in God are challenged. In the midst of my struggles, I lost hope. My faith and relationship with God were tested. God is true to his word when he told us we would be tested in preparation for his kingdom works.

James 1:2–3 said, "My brethren, count it all joy when ye fall into divers' temptations, Knowing this, that the trying of your faith worketh patience." Trials and tribulations are painful; they make us resentful, bitter, and angry. It is during these times that we want to quit and give up; we struggle to continue on with life. If we allow God, he accomplishes the most in our lives during the most difficult times. This book shares how God's grace and mercy provide strength and empowers us to do things we are unable to do on our own. When nothing and no one seemed certain, I found certainty with God. "Jesus Christ the same yesterday, and today, and forever" (Hebrews 13:8). Experiences are an opportunity for spiritual growth and maturity. It is my prayer and hope that through this book and my personal journey, others that know Jesus will have their hope and faith restored. For those that don't know Jesus Christ, I am prayerful that they will accept him as their personal Savior. I believe the greatest gift in life is "being blessed to be a blessing to others."

FOREWORD

Why me, God? That question has been asked by those of us who have experienced pain, struggles, heartaches, rejection, and setbacks that has rocked you to your very core. As the pain engulfs you and you find it hard to breathe, you ask again, "Why me, God? Where are you, God? This is not fair! Like a glass shattering on the floor, you feel your life splintering, and you don't have the strength to pick up the pieces. And not only you but everyone around you gets cut by the broken pieces you still carry.

What if I told you that for every tear, every heartache, every disappointment, and every blow were designed to grow you, to make you stronger, wiser, and better so that God could use you for His glory. Whenever you break a bone, doctors say the broken bone grows back stronger than it was before it was broken. It's in that broken place, when you are weak, God is made strong.

When you feel alone, God is right there by your side. When you can't see, your way, God is your guide. So, when you come out on the other side because you will come out, you realize, just like there is indescribable pain and suffering in my brokenness, there is also a God who will never leave me nor forsake me. Sometimes, we don't understand it, and we can't see it, but all things do work together for our good, and sometimes, God does have to break me before He can bless me!

Pastor Jerry Brown
of Lifeline Church

INTRODUCTION

Experiences change lives. We often grow and evolve into stronger and more confident and courageous individuals as our knowledge increases from life experiences. This book shares traumatic experiences that not only changed my life but also strengthened my relationship with God. After experiencing losses in my life, I was broken and I questioned God, not understanding how or why God allowed these things to happen. I was angry believing the plan God had for my life had changed, wondering how I was supposed to go on with life. Through my study of God's word, I learned that even in the midst of tragedy, God was with me and the plan God had for my life remained the same.

In Isaiah 41:10, God reminds us that he is with us. "Fear thou not; for I am with thee: be not dismayed; for I am thy God: I will strengthen thee; yea I will help thee; yea, I will hold thee with the right hand of my righteousness." God's plan for us developed in the womb. "Before I formed thee in the belly I knew thee; and before thou camest forth of the womb I sanctified thee, and I ordained thee a prophet unto the nations" (Jeremiah 1:5).

When we struggle, we feel that God has abandoned us and he is not with us. Often, its difficult to believe in someone we cannot see in the flesh, hear, touch, or feel; yet we are willing to place our trust in someone or something that has not committed to us as God committed to us in Hebrews 13:5, "God will never leave thee, nor forsake thee."

The darkest times can make one question every fiber of their being, their belief in God, and their salvation, as one may feel lost or even as if they are drowning without a life jacket. Through this book, it's my hope and prayer that others learn that no matter what the

15

tragedy, situation, or circumstance, you have a permanent life jacket if you accept Jesus Christ as your personal Savior. From brokenness and despair, God's grace will take you from "pain to his promise."

1

SACRIFICE

I am the youngest of two children who was born and raised in a small community in South Mississippi. My sister Robin was nearly six years older than me. I had a good childhood. Our family was not wealthy, not even middle class. We had issues and concerns as most families. My parents both worked outside the home. They were both hard workers but neither had a college education; however, education was a necessity. We were raised in the church and taught Christian values and to show the love of God to others. In Matthew 5:43–44, King James Version, it speaks of "loving thy neighbor, and hate thine enemy, but I say unto you, Love your enemies, bless them that curse you, do good to them that hate you, and pray for them which despitefully use you, and persecute you."

Throughout our upbringing, I remember being taught that character reflects behavior. Being independent from God, we could not love our enemies. This type of love comes from God. I believe in the old African proverb: "It takes a village to raise a child." The support of our grandparents, small community, and church family was an influential part of our lives. Our values and beliefs were reinforced by our family and church family.

I grew up in a time that has almost become foreign to most of us—a time when you left your doors unlocked. Everyone in the community knew everyone; your grandparents, uncles, aunts, and cousins lived in walking distance. Neighbors looked out for one another and were often extended family. Sunday worship and fellowship was the highlight of the week.

Your mother was known in the church and community for her kind and generous spirit; her southern cooking was loved by many. Her red beans and rice and pig feet were favorites. And church members raved over her blueberry cake reserved for special church gatherings. We can't forget her famous candy apples. Mama had a generous spirit that was extended to many. I remember her best friend, we called her "Granny," who was like an older sister to her and like a grandmother to Robin and me, died and Mama became a second mom to her daughter, Renee. She was like a grandmother to many children. There were even clothes and toys at our house for the children who referred to her as "BeeBee." In the community, she was known as Ms. Annie B.

My dad was known for his stern demeanor, infrequent smiles, and one-finger handwave when seen in public. Even though Daddy was a man of few words, he was known for his craftsmanship and love for cows and country living. When the children were visiting, he didn't engage much, but you knew he enjoyed them being there. When they were gone, he wanted to know when they would return. Those were the days—the days of sacrifice!

In 1992, while in my junior year of high school, life took an unexpected turn for our family. My dad, a man who didn't miss work and was never sick, became ill with extreme back pain and was hospitalized. My sister was away in graduate school in Louisiana. Daddy was in the hospital several days as doctor's ran test after test until determining that a bone biopsy was needed. A day or so later, we received the results it was cancer multiple myeloma. We were puzzled: "how, what is this, what's the prognosis." The answers to the how and what would come later. According to Mom, the prognosis was good as it was benign: no progression, no chemotherapy, and no radiation needed at this time. Daddy was quiet. He didn't want to discuss it. He seemed withdrawn and in denial. Daddy insisted that no one knew, and we go on with life as usual. While we respected Daddy's wish, it was difficult to ignore what could potentially be ahead for him. It was scary!

We had to know more about multiple myeloma. Robin and I independently researched the disease. Multiple myeloma is rare, and it affects African–Americans more than any other group and is most common in males. It is related to lymphoma and leukemia. After non-Hodgkin lymphoma it is the most common blood cancer. Multiple myeloma is a cancer of the plasma cells of the bone marrow. Cancer cells build up in the bone marrow crowding out healthy blood cells. Chemicals are released from the plasma cells that dissolve bone. The white blood cells normally make antibodies that fight infection; in multiple myeloma, they fight against the body-releasing protein into the bones and blood. With the progression of the disease, the plasma cells seep out the bone marrow spreading throughout the body. Most people live at least five years after the diagnosis. There is no cure. I was unsure how to process this. I found the easiest way to cope was to live in denial. For a period of time, we all joined Daddy in his denial and continued to live life as we did prior to cancer.

Mama and Daddy were examples of how God wants his people to sacrifice to fulfill the works of God's kingdom and for one another. "But to do good and to communicate forget not; for with such sacrifices God is well pleased" (Hebrews 13:16). They often sacrificed their needs and wants for Robin and me. Because of their selflessness and sacrifice, Robin graduated from graduate school, and I graduated high school a year after his diagnosis. Throughout Robin's graduate and undergraduate studies, many financial sacrifices were made for her to attend and graduate from college. They never complained, they reminded Robin that her hard work would pay off. I knew the bar had been set, and I could not disappoint. I would begin college in the fall.

I stayed home my freshman year and went to junior college, and Robin began working at a university. Daddy and Mama continued working as usual. Daddy was a workaholic. His work did not stop after his full-time job was done; he stayed busy with working odd jobs and his hobbies.

During my freshman year my maternal grandmother, "Nanny" suffered a stroke. A few months later, Nanny suffered a fatal heart attack. During my Nanny's sickness and death, Mama's faith never wavered; her commitment to God and his work continued. Mama and her family were no strangers to grief and loss. Prior to Nanny's death, Mama had lost two sisters and a brother. Even in her grief, she reminded us that God was a just God, "That ye may be the children of your Father which is in heaven for he maketh his sun to rise on the evil and on the good, and sendeth rain on the just and on the unjust" (Matthew 5:45).

Mama reminded us that in life, we all will go through trials and tribulations—the saved and the unsaved. When we go through trials, this is God preparing you for greater works. She knew that God had greater works for her, so in her grief, she continued to be active in the church, singing in the choir, and serving as a deaconess, usher, and church financial secretary.

The next fall, I went off to college in Alabama to begin my sophomore year. This was an exciting time—new experiences, new people, and most importantly, independence. With independence, responsibilities increased. I had some adult responsibilities: motivating myself to get up and ready for class, studying, working, cooking, doing my own laundry, and maintaining my student housing.

I had a cousin, his wife, and two sons who lived in the area. His boys were also my God brothers. I frequently visited them during my college years. I was able to get a "free" homecooked meal and "free" laundry services. My cousin pastored a church near campus, so I was able to attend Sunday worship service with family and others familiar to me. In my teenage years, I visited my cousin and his family regularly and was familiar with some members of his church family.

Throughout college I was fortunate to work for a local insurance agency. I began learning the insurance industry while in high school. A friend's mom gave me a job at her insurance agency during my junior year of high school, and I worked there until I left home for college. Little did I know this part-time job in insurance would serve me well later. By the end of the first semester, I had adjusted well. The daily phone calls with Mama and her frequent care packages helped with my adjustment. She was always thoughtful, sending me my favorite snacks, a little cash, and always something special and unexpected. I remember receiving a radio I had been wanting one Valentine's Day. I could always count on Mama to lift my spirits. Initially, I thought all college students had the support of their parents. I was surprised to learn that some college students were totally self-sufficient. Scholarships, grants, student loans, and work study were their only sources of financial support, and there was no one calling daily or sending care packages. I realized I was somewhat naive and was not as independent as I thought.

2

PATIENCE

When I came home from college, things seemed the same. The cancer was never discussed. Daddy looked healthy as ever; he had even gained a little weight. He was still working and doing all the activities he enjoyed: riding the tractor, baling hay, and tending to the cows. I remember him being excited about buying a round hay baler.

If it were baseball season, Mama was consumed with watching America's game. She was always excited for the start of baseball and to watch her favorite team, the LA Dodgers. Mama always prepared one of my favorite meals while I was home: fried shrimp and red beans and rice. It was not until I left home that I realized the value and importance of home. I missed Mama's cooking and our girl time together, my church family, and visiting my grandparents next door.

Growing up, my grandparents were an influential part of my life. I had lived next door to them my entire life. I visited my grandparents nearly daily "just because." When I was a little girl, my grandfather would meet me at the bus stop in the afternoons and would take me for a "hamburger and cold drink." In the winter, he would make a fire in the fireplace, so I would be warm while waiting on Mama and Daddy to come home from work. I was considered a latchkey kid. Robin was not usually home until later, because she was involved in after school activities. Coming home reminded me of childhood memories that contributed to the person I am now.

I recall looking forward to going home to visit during spring break. I was midway in the second semester of my sophomore year. I had pledged into a sorority early spring. I was celebrating my twentieth birthday and was looking forward to attending my first sorority regional conference. I knew this visit would be a joyous time, because when I got home, Mama would have had a birthday cake made and would have plans to celebrate my birthday. No matter where Robin or I was or what we were doing, Mama always found a way for us to celebrate our birthdays, and a cake was always a part of the celebration. While I was away at school, an uncle had moved in temporarily with my parents.

When I arrived home, as expected, I had a beautiful birthday cake waiting for me, decorated with pastel roses in my sorority colors. Mama was always attentive to detail.

The tone of the visit abruptly changed. During my visit, I found medical supplies, which disturbed me. Mama was at work, so I spoke with my uncle about my findings. Without a pause or hesitation, he encouraged me to speak with my mother.

I spoke with Mama later that evening about the medical supplies. She reluctantly told me Daddy had started chemotherapy and radiation. The medical supplies were to clean his stent which was used to administer the chemotherapy. The cancer was malignant and had begun to spread. He was now going to chemotherapy and radiation weekly, experiencing manageable side effects. He was even returning to work after his treatments. She explained that he chose not to be treated locally and was being treated by an oncologist approximately forty-five minutes north of our hometown.

Just as I was unaware, my sister was also unaware of the progression of the cancer. He continued to keep his diagnosis a secret from family and friends. Finally, Mama admitted the weight of the disease was too much for her to manage alone. She confided in my dad's oldest sister, Eva.

Eva became a support and confidant for Mom. Even though Eva lived six hours away in the suburbs outside Atlanta, she visited and maintained regular contact. It was hard to keep this secret considering my dad was from a large family. He was one of eleven children and the oldest child to my grandmother and second oldest child to my grandfather. To his siblings, he was the patriarch of the family as he worked and assisted in the care of his younger siblings while in high school. He had a close relationship with both parents but was extremely close to his mother. The diagnosis would devastate her. With my paternal grandparents living next door, he visited them daily. Daddy seemed to not allow the chemotherapy to visibly affect him. He continued to visit his parents daily and spent most Saturdays either in the country visiting his favorite aunt and tending to her property and their cattle or with his closest friend who is a deacon at the church. While undergoing treatment, he continued to serve as a deacon. I was uncertain, but I felt he likely confided in his best friend and two of his five sisters that he had been diagnosed with cancer.

Returning to school after that visit was initially a challenge. For the first time, the gravity of his condition was slowly becoming a reality. It had been four years since his initial diagnosis and all had seemed well. I questioned how did I not know the cancer had become malignant. I wondered when it became malignant. When did he start chemotherapy and radiation? When I asked these questions, both Mama and Daddy were vague. They both acted as if my questions were irrelevant. Mama reminded me that we had to trust God. I remember her quoting a well-known Scripture, Psalm 55:22: "Cast thy burden upon the Lord, and he shall sustain thee: he shall never suffer the righteous to be moved."

Daddy insisted he was doing well and denied any adverse side effects from the treatments. He physically appeared healthy and behaved as usual. I wonder if I was so self-absorbed with anticipating college graduation and planning my future that I was oblivious to what was going on at home. While back at school, I began to do more research on multiple myeloma. It was a rare form of cancer with a survival rate of 29.6%. There is no definitive cause of multiple myeloma, but it is suspected that certain environmental exposures may be the cause of multiple myeloma. After learning a little more about multiple myeloma, I felt I had more questions than answers. How was it possible for someone who never drank, smoked, or use any illicit substances or engaged in any high-risk behaviors to have obtained such a rare form of cancer? There was no rational explanation. I placed my trust in God and believed Daddy would beat the cancer.

A year and a half had passed since Robin and I learned Daddy was undergoing cancer treatments. I had visited home multiple times since the previous spring and, on occasions, spent a week or two at home during an extended break.

In early summer 1997, I received a call from my Aunt Eva saying that I needed to come home. She said Daddy had been in the hospital for several days. He is now home but is not doing well. I was in summer school, so I packed up to come home for the weekend. When I arrived home, he was weak and frail; the mood was somber. I learned, as suspected, that Daddy had shared with at least one of his two sisters that he had cancer. Daddy had shared his diagnosis with Aunt Eva several years prior. The secret remained between the five us: Daddy, Mama, Aunt Eva, Robin, and me.

It was difficult to witness his declining health and increasingly difficult to keep his diagnosis a secret. Mama was always our "rock" and "strength." Her behaviors were always a reflection of her character. I was concerned as to Daddy's prognosis. He had experienced significant weight loss and physically and emotionally appeared tired. Although he was always a man of few words, he said even less.

When I shared my concerns with Mama, she reminded me of her favorite Scripture: "Let not your heart be troubled; ye believe in God also believe in me" (John 14:1). In her words, "trust God." She reminded me as I attempted to understand why and how that God will provide understanding in his time, and we must not question God but be obedient. As I tried to wrap my mind around what I thought was happening and what was unspoken, I was becoming emotionally numb. I felt Daddy was dying, and no one was saying anything. At the end of the weekend, Mama and Daddy insisted I return to school.

I returned to school to finish summer school. Shortly after returning, I received a phone call saying that I needed to come home; specifically, I was told to come to the hospital. I was told his conditioned had worsened, and he was back in the hospital. I drove over three hundred and fifty miles and over five hours alone. He was hospitalized in Hattiesburg, Mississippi, in the same town where he received treatment. I was physically alone, but I knew God was with me. At the age of twelve, I accepted Jesus Christ as my personal Savior. During my teenage and young adult years, I was not living according to God's word; I was spiritually immature. I was not in a relationship with God. I believed in God, but he was not Lord of my life. When God is not Lord of our life, we are not living explicitly for him. We treat God like a spare tire; we only use God when we need him. I needed God, and I remember reaching out to him during my drive to the hospital. I was asking God for healing.

When I arrived at the hospital, it was odd. My mother met me in the parking lot. In those days, there was no texting and cell phones were only used for an emergency. She watched for my arrival from the window of Daddy's hospital room. For the first time since the initial diagnosis, I heard the pain in her voice and saw the tears in her eyes. I remember us walking into the hospital lobby arm in arm; we sat and talked. She told me that Robin was on a flight, and she would arrive in a few hours. I felt my heart sank. I knew the prognosis was not good. She said the three of us have decisions to make.

Daddy was in renal failure. The cancer had spread and was affecting his kidney function. She said that the options were limited. Without dialysis, he would have eight to ten days to live. With dialysis, they would begin a "new" chemotherapy treatment and radiation; this was the only treatment option. If his body did not respond, death was inevitable.

For him to begin dialysis, he would have a minor surgical procedure in which they would insert a catheter in a large vein in his neck. Physically and mentally, he was declining. He was no longer able to make decisions for himself due to confusion. I was devastated when I saw him—he was thin and frail, and his eyes were sunken and appeared more tired than he did during my last visit. I had never seen him like this before.

He smiled when he saw me; his words were few. We waited together for Robin to arrive. Later that evening, Robin arrived. The three of us spoke outside his room. Daddy was aware of his prognosis and the recommendations of his oncologist. Early on in his treatment, he had discussed with the oncologist as the cancer progressed to continue to advise him of the prognosis and any recommendations. We prayed and asked God for guidance and peace and for his will to be done.

For me, it was difficult to ask for God's will to be done and not my will. My will was complete healing and restoration of the flesh. I was selfish. Daddy was too young. He wouldn't see me graduate from college, get married, or have children.

It was decided that he would have the surgical procedure to begin dialysis. I remember being touched that his oncologist asked to pray with us. The oncologist told us over the course of treating Daddy that they had spoken about their faith, religion, and belief in God.

I thought to myself, *"It's a blessing that Daddy's physician was a Christian."*

He tried to reassure us we made the best decision for Daddy to be able to move forward with treatment.

The time had come to let family and friends know what was ahead. We first told Daddy's siblings, and they collectively decided that they would tell my grandparents. They were devastated. Daddy was grandma's first born and they had a true mother–son bond. As the word began to spread throughout the family and community, the support became overwhelming. In hindsight, God's grace and mercy surrounded us.

"But he giveth more grace Wherefore he saith, God resisteth the proud, but giveth grace unto the humble" (James 4:6).

God's grace cost nothing; he gives it freely. Robin struggled with leaving as she had to return to work in a few days. I had to return to school. Mama would be on family medical leave without pay. It would be a financial strain with no household income. Mama would be left without the physical and emotional support of "my girls," as she sometimes called us. Her strength mesmerized me as she assured us with a Scripture, Romans 8:28: "And we know that all things work together for good to them that love God, to them who are called according to his purpose." I knew I was spiritually immature as I tried to believe in the Scriptures Mama referenced while witnessing her walk in her faith.

Family, church family, and friends were in and out visiting. Robin returned to North Carolina. Out-of-town relatives traveled to visit over the course of his extensive hospital stay. His "baby sister" Eloise, who was serving in the US Army, was deployed to Bosnia during this time. I remember her calling as frequently as she could. Of the first to visit was two of Daddy's sisters Rose and Ann from Chicago. I was preparing to leave soon and return to Alabama to finish summer school and for work.

During the visit, Aunt Rose offered to pay my housing expense in order for me to leave my job for the summer to help Mama with Daddy. She shared with me how Daddy helped her financially when she was in college and that she was glad to do for me what he had done for her. I accepted her offer and immediately began making arrangements to be home for the summer. I had to return to Alabama to secure my housing and speak with my professor and my employer. Both were willing and made accommodations for me to be away for the remainder of the summer semester.

Throughout that summer, Robin would visit. Mama's coworkers arranged to work their weekly off day, and in return, Mama would be paid as if she were working. She was off work for an extended period of time caring for Daddy and never missed a paycheck. For weeks, Daddy was in the hospital. Between family and Daddy's closest friends, he never physically spent a day or night alone in the hospital. Someone was always there to see him off, whether it was to dialysis, chemotherapy, or radiation, and someone was always waiting for him to return.

Mama's biological father, stepmother, and four siblings resided in close proximity to the hospital. She had a somewhat distant relationship with her father. Her parents divorced when she was young, and her mother remarried. Until I was nine years old, I thought Mama's stepfather was her biological father. Even as an adult, Mama had infrequent visits with her dad. God has a way in which he brings people together just as he brought the Jews and Gentiles together. My grandfather and step-grandmother's house burned prior to Daddy experiencing complications from cancer.

Without insurance, Daddy arranged with volunteers to rebuild their home primarily with donated supplies and volunteer labor. They would often reward Daddy and the work crew with lunch and dinner.

In Genesis 22:11–14, God tells Abraham to offer his only son Isaac for a burnt offering. Abraham is obedient and takes Isaac and offers him for a burnt offering. God then tells Abraham to remove his hand from Isaac and not lay him for a burnt offering; he was being tested. He feared God. When Abraham lifted up his eyes, he saw a ram and gave the ram for a burnt offering.

"God always has a ram in the bush." Throughout Daddy's hospital stay, Mama's father, stepmother, and siblings were there providing support and offering words of encouragement. God created an opportunity for broken relationships to be mended.

On occasion, we stayed in a nearby hotel as opposed to driving the forty-five minutes home late at night and to have time away from the hospital. Some days, we drove home and back to the hospital a few times in a day. Mama didn't like to drive, so I was the designated driver. I frequently played the song "Your Grace and Mercy."

It was nothing but God's grace and mercy that placed these individuals in our lives and allowed them to provide something for us that we were unable to provide for ourselves. God has the power to work through someone else to bless you. In the book of Genesis, God blesses Lot through the generosity of Abram. Abram later became Abraham. Abram knew that by trusting and obeying God, he would take care of him.

"Now the Lord had said unto Abram Get thee out of thy country, and from thy kindred and from thy father's house, unto a land that I will show thee. And I will make of thee a great nation, and I will bless thee and make thy name great; and thou shalt be a blessing: And I will bless them that bless thee" (Genesis 12:1–3).

Although I was familiar with Scripture and saw God's grace and mercy demonstrated, I continued to feel spiritually weak. Unconsciously, I questioned God.

It would take weeks before we knew whether or not his body was responding to the chemotherapy and radiation. He would have to continue the dialysis until it was time for a reevaluation of the cancer. Some days were long and hard; it was difficult to witness him in immense pain. He was never one to complain, and even at his worse, he didn't complain. Over the weeks, we were receiving daily visits from the oncologist.

I remember on one of the visits, the oncologist notified us that his red blood cell count was dropping, and if it continued he would need a blood transfusion. His blood count continued to drop; he needed a blood transfusion. Our church family coordinated with a local blood bank and held a blood drive at the church. The community, family, and friends came out, donated blood, and supported us. The outpouring support continued to be overwhelming. It was another example of God's grace. Daddy was given blood to increase his red blood cell count. I was feeling optimistic!

3

PEACE

It had been over a month now, and he was continuing to undergo chemotherapy and dialysis. The oncologist met with the four of us and told us his body was not responding to chemotherapy. He recommended discontinuing dialysis. The cancer was spreading, and there were no other treatment options. Once dialysis ceased, he would experience renal failure and life expectancy would be eight to ten days.

I remembered we were heartbroken; there was silence. I felt immense pain that Daddy knew he was given days to live. In the coming days, he requested certain individuals to visit. There were constant visits and prayers. I remember, around the fifth day without dialysis, his confusion worsened. He became upset, pulling out his intravenous lines. He shouted that it didn't matter, "I'm going to die anyway." It was awful to hear him say those words and to know it was true. Within a few minutes, we were able to calm him. He was not one to say, "I love you," but he told us he loved us and wished he had lived life more and worked less.

On the eighth day July 19, at approximately 11:00 p.m., we were summoned from the family waiting room to Daddy's room by the nurse. She advised that he had about an hour to live. The nurse explained the signs of death, which included labored breathing and a distinct smell. The nurse encouraged us to talk to him and; provide comfort and encouragement to assist him with transitioning as he would leave his earthly body. She explained that sometimes, when dying, an individual needs to be told by loved ones that it's okay to die. She explained that if we knew something he might be holding on to, it would be beneficial to assure him that it would be okay.

Mama was overcome with emotions. She cried and said she was unable to talk him through death and dying. We all agreed that he was likely worried that I would not finish college. He felt it was his responsibility that Robin and I obtained a college degree. Throughout our teenage years, he reiterated the importance of education and the ability to be self-sufficient. The three us went into his room— Mama with tears, and Robin and I were numb. I was overcome with the smell of death as his bodily organs were shutting down. Robin stood to his right, and I stood to his left.

We held his hands, and we let him know that we would all meet again someday. Robin assured him that it was okay to be at peace and that I would finish college. We told him we loved him and we would be okay, and it was okay to let go and rest. He took his final breath, and he was gone to be with our heavenly father at 11:30 p.m.

Daddy had fought long and hard. "I have fought a good fight, I have finished my course, I have kept the faith" (2 Timothy 4:7). We cried and held each other in his room for a while. Robin and I began to make phone calls to family and Daddy's best friend. Within minutes, three of Mama's siblings and Daddy's best friend had arrived. We left the room, so his friend and one of Mama's brothers could be alone with Daddy and say their goodbyes. Once all the goodbyes were said, Mama's siblings packed up all of his belongings and drove us home.

It was early the next morning when we arrived home. We did not sleep much as we prepared to receive visitors later that day. It was Sunday, so we expected visitors after church service. I vaguely remember the comings and goings of that day. People called, visited, brought food, and extended their condolences. The day was a blur, as I was still numb and in disbelief.

I particularly remember a close high-school friend coming to visit, Felice. Felice and I bonded following the tragic death of a mutual friend and high-school classmate. Her visit was one of the few I remember because we visited and chatted like old times. Often, when someone dies, people struggle with words, and there is a clear awkwardness to engage. With Felice, there was no awkwardness, just a friend supporting another friend.

That day, Mama worked on the obituary along with church members. This was one of her responsibilities in the church assisting families with obituaries in their time of bereavement. Everything was moving fast. The next day, we travelled to the funeral home to make funeral arrangements in preparation for our final goodbyes.

Fortunately, Mama had obtained burial insurance for her and Daddy years prior. This was one less financial stressor. The services were scheduled: visitation would be Friday and the funeral would be Saturday. I remember we agreed on a faded navy-blue casket with light blue interior; it was beautiful. The casket spray ordered was various shades of fresh yellow flowers, including yellow roses and carnations. Mama made sure the floral director knew she wanted it to completely cover a large area of the casket. The obituary was taken to a local printer we had known for years. It was arranged for Daddy's cousin, Pastor Davis, to give the eulogy. It was important to Mama that everything was perfect for Daddy's homegoing.

It all seemed surreal, and I was just physically going through the motions. Friday had come, and I knew it would be a long weekend. That Friday evening, the visitation was held. We greeted visitors throughout the evening. The following day were the funeral services. The church was full. Some of my college friends and sorority sisters came from Alabama. His homegoing celebration was beautiful.

I remember during the eulogy, Pastor Davis spoke of his relationship with Daddy. He shared how he always knew when he was the student and Daddy was the teacher and when he was the teacher and Daddy was the student. When Daddy called him by his first name "Wendell," he was the student, but when he referred to him as "Pastor Davis," he was the teacher and Daddy was the student.

After the service, everyone gathered in the fellowship hall of the church for repass. Repass is a gathering of family and friends following a funeral service where dinner is served. Due to heavy rain, his burial was postponed to Monday. On Monday, a neighbor who was a highway patrol offered to lead the procession to the cemetery. Grandma had a hard time saying goodbye to her firstborn son. We all cried as they lowered his casket to the final resting place. I found some comfort in knowing that he was no longer in pain and that as God promised in his word we would meet again.

Paul offers words of comfort in 1 Thessalonians 4:13–18 because he does not want those left after loved ones are deceased to be ignorant to God's promise "But I would not have you to be ignorant, brethren, concerning them which are sleep, that ye sorrow not, even as others which have no hope. For if we believe that Jesus died and rose again, even so them also which sleep in Jesus will God bring with him. For this we say unto you by the word of the Lord, that we which are alive and remain unto the coming of the Lord shall not prevent them which are asleep. For the Lord himself shall descend from the heaven with a shout, with the voice of the archangel, and with the trump of God; and the dead in Christ shall rise first: Then we which are alive and remain shall be caught up together with them in the clouds, to meet with the Lord in the air; and so shall we ever be with the Lord. Wherefore comfort one another with these words."

The following days, everyone would return to their respective homes and my life was forever changed. Robin would remain home for a week or so before having to return to work. I had a few weeks before fall semester would start. During this time, we helped Mama begin the process of settling his affairs. We were comforted that Mama would not be home alone; her brother was still in the home and would be able to assist her. In addition, my paternal grandparents were next door and family and friends would continue to support her. Robin left to return to North Carolina. Shortly after, I returned to Alabama.

I remember the six-hour drive back seemed like an eternity. I cried nearly the entire time, overwhelmed with emotions. I returned to work immediately and begin completing work for the summer school course I was taking prior to leaving for Mississippi. I was able to complete all summer school course work prior to the start of the fall semester. My daily calls with Mama increased from a couple times daily to about three or four times a day. Throughout the semester, I made more frequent visits home.

During one of my visits, I took Mama to work. We stopped by the cemetery on the way. The headstone was done, and a floral arrangement sat in the vase. I was somewhat taken by the headstone; it was a double headstone with our family name and both names and birth dates engraved. Of course, Daddy's death date was engraved, and a space was left open for Mama's death date. As we stood at the grave talking, I learned Mama visited the cemetery daily. I was concerned with how she was coping, but I myself was not coping well. I was living in denial.

She explained that after thirty years of marriage, there was an emptiness and a void she was unable to fill. I believe we were just going through the motions of living, searching for our "new normal," and some sense of earthly peace. Mama was now visiting my paternal grandparents daily just as Daddy did and making sure their basic needs were met. She often prepared dinner for them and ran errands, if needed. I believe this was her way of trying to fill the void.

My grandmother often referred to my mother as her Ruth. She was referring to the Biblical story of Naomi and Ruth. Ruth was Naomi's daughter-in-law, and when Ruth's husband which was Naomi's son died, Naomi instructed Ruth to return to the land of Judah to her mother's house. "And Ruth said, Entreat me not to leave thee, or to return from following after thee: for whither thou goest, I will go; and where thou lodgest, I will lodge: thy people shall be my people, and thy God my God" (Ruth 1:16).

Just as Ruth took care of Naomi and did not leave her, Mama took care of my grandparents and did not leave them. She was more of a daughter than a daughter-in-law. I believe caring for my grandparents for her was an extension of Daddy and honoring his memory. Of my grandparents surviving ten children, five boys and five girls, all of the girls lived out of state. The girls seemed appreciative of Mama's love and dedication to their parents. Frequently, they called or sent gifts of thanks.

CHAPTER

4

DENIAL

Seconds, minutes, hours, days, weeks, and months passed, and I had learned to use compartmentalization to hide my emotional pain from others. Each aspect of my life had its own compartment, and I made a concerted effort to not have them overlap. I was more focused than ever to complete school. I had four semesters left before graduation. I graduated with a bachelor of arts degree in December 1998. I consumed myself with distractions to avoid my emotional pain.

Between work and school, attending church, and remaining involved in the sorority, my days and evenings were full. Time was passing! I was clearly in denial. Denial gave me the ability to go on with life, doing what was required while in an emotionally numb state. When I was alone at night, I found myself struggling to make sense of it all. I had not envisioned a life without one of my parents. I knew that tomorrow was not promised and that just as we have a birthday, we have a death day, but I believed both my parents would live to see me accomplish all the milestones I hoped to accomplish: college graduation, marriage, evolving into my career, purchasing my first home and my first car, and becoming a mother and a grandmother. I felt I was cheated.

Even though I was a Christian, I begin to find it increasingly difficult to pray. I knew I was to trust God. I had witnessed his grace and mercy throughout Daddy's illness, but I grappled to understand. Why my father? He was a good person. Why do bad things happen to good people? Remembering what I had been taught, I knew questioning God was unacceptable, but the flesh can be weak.

I had difficulty controlling my negative thoughts. I guarded my thoughts and feelings, not saying much to anyone. When grieving the loss of a loved one, there are common questions from others: "How are you doing" or "Do you need anything?" I began to despise these questions. When asked, I would internally grit my teeth and give my classic response with a half-smile, "I'm okay." In reality, I was thinking, *"Does the person really want to know how I am or are they asking to be courteous?"*

"How are you doing," and "do you need anything" are loaded questions, and people ask these questions often not recognizing the potential outcome. I often thought, *"If I answered them honestly and unloaded with how I really felt and what I really needed, the person asking would be overwhelmed with disbelief."*

God knew I was in denial and withdrawing myself from others. At the time, I did not realize that denial was part of the grieving and healing process. God is an on-time God, sending what I needed when I needed it. I frequently received cards of encouragement from Mama and sometimes a card from Robin. I was not being transparent in sharing my thoughts with them, but I know they knew the pain I was experiencing as they were experiencing pain as well. Mama made sure to send a card of encouragement on Daddy's birthday which was less than two months after his death. I did not realize how difficult birthdays, anniversaries, and holidays would become now that Daddy is gone.

The semester had ended; five months had past and it was our first Christmas without Daddy. Daddy was never one for the holidays, but Mama loved Christmas. Robin and I were both home for Christmas. Mama had several Christmas traditions with us, and she continued those traditions. Even as young adults, Robin and I were required to give Mama a Christmas list a few months prior to Christmas. She and Daddy had to go pick a live Christmas tree. Mama always decorated the tree in a certain color scheme with coordinating wrapping paper. Her Christmas village sat near the Christmas tree. She enjoyed Christmas shopping.

Growing up, we always adopted a child or two off the *Angel Tree*. We did not have a lot, but she reminded us we had more than others. She would take us shopping for gifts for the child or children off the *Angel Tree*. Mama would always purchase items off our Christmas list and then add her special must-haves for us. Stuffing stockings and Christmas dinner were also among our traditions.

During the holiday, Daddy would sit around and observe. On Christmas morning, we were up early. Mama was always the first one awake and the most excited. She would be in the kitchen preparing Christmas dinner. Once Robin and I were awake, we made it into the living room to open gifts. Mama would accompany us, and Daddy would straddle in last as usual. This year was different; it was the three of us and Uncle Gerald. We did things just as we had for the last twenty years, but there was an emptiness without Daddy. We would always visit our grandparents on Christmas morning, and they would always visit us late morning or midafternoon to see our Christmas gifts. This year was no different. Robin and I visited them, and then, they visited us. A few more relatives visited this year.

While home for the holidays, Mama told us we had business we had to attend to, including meeting with an attorney as she was settling Daddy's affairs. We reviewed and signed documents. It felt unreal. Daddy had no health insurance; his hospital bills were over $100,000. Mama received a letter from the hospital stating his hospital bill had been settled and paid in full. This was God's continuous grace.

It was no different, I was sad to be leaving Mama and returning to school. I was just three semesters from graduation. Literally, I was counting down. This semester, I left working for the insurance agency. It was sad but bittersweet. I had worked with the staff for nearly three years, and they had been extremely supportive of me. The owner of the agency was accommodating to my class schedule as much as possible and was a support during the illness and loss of Daddy. I obtained a job working as an assistant to the activities director of a local low-income housing community.

I would be responsible for overseeing a General Equivalence Degree program and assisting with community activities for residents. This experience was much needed as it would allow me to continue in my denial and pour myself into my work and helping others.

I started classes and my new job. My boss was young and enthusiastic. The job was a great fit. I enjoyed getting to know the residents and helping them achieve their goals. The job sparked a light and gave me direction for plans after graduation. I had decided that after graduation, I would obtain employment and purse graduate school part-time. I wanted to obtain a graduate degree in social work.

I was excited. I called and shared my thoughts with Mama. She was happy for me. She asked if I had prayed about a job after graduation and my plan. I told her "yes," but I had not been consistently praying.

"Pray without ceasing" (1 Thessalonians 5:16). She reminded me to pray and that she was praying for me. It is written in 1 Timothy 2:1, "I exhort therefore, that, first of all, supplications, prayers, intercession, and giving of thanks, be made for all men."

Mama was interceding on my behalf by praying to God for me. Her prayers were heard, and God's grace continued on my life.

After church one Sunday, I was stopped by a young man who attended church with me. My cousin, Pastor Davis, was the church pastor and the congregation was relatively large. It was not uncommon to not know a fellow church member. He asked me out on a date. Initially, I said, "no". I questioned his age, thinking he was younger than me. To my surprise, he was three years older than I am. I agreed to a date.

We begin spending time together. Initially, I did not realize I knew his stepmother. I had known his stepmother since I was thirteen years old. As a teenager, I spent summers visiting with my cousin and his family. His stepmother had been a local hairstylist in the community for many years. Eventually Shane and I started dating. Over time, I shared with Shane about the passing of my dad. I was still in denial and compartmentalizing my thoughts and feelings. He was patient with me, allowing me to share on my terms.

Graduation was getting close. It was October 1998, and I had not secured a job post-graduation. A large insurance company was holding a job fair. I was familiar with the company, having worked for two of its agents in the past. I decided to attend hoping to secure employment. Several days following the job fair, I was contacted and given a contingent job offer. The offer was contingent on completing my undergraduate degree. Although I continued to struggle in my relationship with God, I knew this was his will. The experience I had from working in the insurance industry in high school and college had paid off. I accepted the offer knowing I would have to relocate. Both Shane and Mama were excited for me. I would be about an hour and a half from Shane and about four and a half hours from Mama. I scheduled a day of apartment hunting. Shane assisted me in my housing search.

December was here! Mama came for a graduation reception that was held in lieu of commencement which would be held the following May. She was so happy and proud now that both Robin and I had completed college. I remember her laughing and smiling, saying she might go to college now. Even though she said she was joking, I think she really was considering college. It had been a dream and desire of hers for many years.

Following high school, she had been accepted to college and planned to study education, but in those days, a parent signature was required for college admission. Her mother refused to sign the acceptance letter, so Mama put her dreams on hold. I told Mama if she were serious about college, she had the support of me and Robin. She said she would think about it.

The next day, I drove Mama back home to Mississippi. On the way we stopped to see where I would be residing after graduation. Mama loved my apartment and the surrounding community; it was in a quiet secluded area. She felt it would be a safe area for me. It was in close proximity to the mall, grocery stores, eateries, and other businesses. I was super excited—a real grown up totally responsible for myself.

It was close to Christmas, so we planned on Robin and Mama coming to spend Christmas with me. As usual, Robin and I prepared and provided our Christmas list for Mama. This year was a little different as she had Shane prepare a list too. He was surprise as this was something he and his family did not do. Robin had just purchased her first new car. She was going to drive from North Carolina to Mississippi, and then she and Mama would drive to Alabama. After Christmas, they would assist with my move to Birmingham. I was scheduled to begin my new job after Christmas as a fire underwriter for a major insurance company. We all had mixed feelings as this would be our first Christmas ever away from home. Mama was a little concerned about her Christmas traditions and being away from home for the holidays. However, she insisted we have a Christmas tree.

Years prior, she had purchased a Christmas tree for my apartment. Shane and I decorated the small tree. I knew Christmas would be different, but I wanted it as special as it had been for years.

5

STRENGTH

I had completed my Christmas shopping. It was Christmas Eve, and I was spending the day with Shane, while waiting on Mama and Robin to arrive. Robin and Mama had left Mississippi and were headed to visit me for the holidays. I was anxiously awaiting their arrival. Shane and I had dinner with his dad, stepmother, and siblings. It was about 7:00 in the evening when we returned to my apartment. I had not heard from Robin and Mama.

When we arrived at the apartment, I checked to see if I had missed their call. I had not received a call from them. I had a call and message from a hospital that was an hour south of Huntsville. As I listened to the message, my heart began to race. I was told to call the hospital. A male left his name and a number to call. I was shaking as I returned the phone call. I was asked questions to confirm the identify of my mother and sister.

He advised that there had been an accident, and Robin was in critical condition and at their hospital. Mama had suffered severe head trauma and was taken by ambulance to a Birmingham hospital that had a head trauma unit. He explained that they attempted to take Mama by med flight, but the helicopter was unable to land. The day prior, we had had some icy roads throughout north Alabama. The roadways cleared, but as the temperatures dropped that evening, some roadways refroze.

Because of ice, the helicopter was unable to land. I remember clearly my knees buckled, and I fell to the floor with my hands to my face crying. Shane took the phone and got additional information from the gentleman. He told him we would be on our way shortly, explaining we were coming from Huntsville. I could hear the man telling Shane that the roads heading south were treacherous and to take our time and be careful. I remember Shane helping me pack clothes. He called his parents and told them what happened and that he was taking me to the hospital. It seemed as if it took hours to get to the hospital.

In route, I was praying and initially questioning why God allowed this to happen. I quickly realized, there was no time to dwell on why. I went it to survival mode. I made phone calls notifying family of the accident. I first called Uncle Gerald and asked that he go to Birmingham to be with Mama. Both Mama and Robin were critical. I didn't know if Mama would make it through the night, and I didn't want her to die alone. I told him I was headed to be with Robin because the hospital where she was was in closer proximity to me. I would have to pass Robin to get to Mama.

Once I assessed the situation with Robin, I would be headed to Birmingham, but I needed someone to be with Mama until I arrived. Uncle Gerald seemed as shocked as I was. Mama was his big sister and became a second mother after their mother died. He agreed that he would be heading to Birmingham and would call with an update once he arrived. It would take him at least four-and-a-half hours to get to Birmingham. I spoke with Daddy's youngest brother Uncle Michael and asked that he share with the family. I also spoke with Renee and ask that she share with her daddy, Uncle John, and others in our church family. Uncle John was like a grandfather and was the senior deacon in the church. Uncle John was the church member who everyone relied on for strength and encouragement. He was that person who knew and lived the word of God. He exemplified the character of a Christian.

I finally arrived at the hospital. I was taken to Robin, and she was still being evaluated. She was conscious with contusions and abrasion all over and a broken pelvis. Robin was able to speak with me briefly before they placed a tube through her nose to monitor her overnight for internal bleeding. She sobbed as she tried to explain what had happened. I understood her saying she and Mama were outside the vehicle. She then repeatedly stated, "He just hit us, Ashley. He just hit us." I didn't tell her anything about Mama at that time. I tried to comfort her as best I could. The nurse advised me that they would be placing her in a room. I spoke with the highway patrol at the hospital about the accident. He explained to me Robin was driving, and they were northbound. Robin lost control of the vehicle on an icy bridge while another vehicle approached the bridge and lost control, and the two vehicles collided. Robin and Mama were okay from the initial accident. They had gotten out of the vehicle and were on the shoulder of the road preparing to get behind the guardrail when a vehicle traveling northbound lost control of his vehicle on the icy bridge, spun around backwards, and hit Robin and Mama, knocking them over the guardrail.

According to a witness, the driver got out of his vehicle, looked at what he had done, and left the scene. The witness spoke with the man and tried to reason with him to remain at the scene, but he fled. It is believed that Mama suffered the majority of the impact from the out-of-control vehicle. The accident was considered a hit and run. The highway patrolman explained they were investigating. He encouraged me to wait until morning to travel to Birmingham due to road conditions.

I told Robin that Uncle Gerald was going to be with Mama, and Shane and I would head to Birmingham later tonight once she was more stable. I was numb thinking how I would go on without Mama, my best friend. I had lost one "lifeline," Daddy, and I was overcome with the thoughts of losing my last lifeline. Mama and I had always had an unbreakable bond. Family and friends often reminded me as a baby and young child I clung to my Mama.

Even as a young adult, I still enjoyed cuddling and sitting in Mama's lap. If I lost her, how would I go on? It had only been one year, five month, and five days since we lost Daddy. I had to contain my emotions, because Robin needed me. Shane stayed with me; he never left. We spent the night in Robin's room as nurses were in and out throughout the night monitoring her to ensure she remained stable. I woke up early the next morning; it was Christmas Day. I realized Uncle Gerald had not called with an update on Mama. I went to the nurses' station to use the phone. The nurse provided me with a list of names and numbers. She explained people had been calling for me throughout the night, and she thought it was best that I rest as I would have long days ahead. I thanked her for her concern. She provided me with the messages; there was no call or message from Uncle Gerald. I called Uncle Gerald, and he was vague and provided no information on Mama other than that he was at the hospital, and he had been with her throughout the night. I told him I would be heading there shortly. I was concerned with leaving Robin alone. Shane spoke with his parents, and they advised they would be coming to the hospital today to stay with Robin, relieving us to go to Birmingham.

I felt as if I was traveling an unfamiliar road and it was storming and I could not see nor had any idea what was ahead. It was a blur! But God! Just as God surrounded us with his grace and mercy during Daddy's illness, he surrounded us now. Shane and I left for Birmingham. The road conditions were rough. We ran into a number of areas of patchy ice. I remember a vehicle lost control in front of us and went off the shoulder of the road. Shane stopped to offer help. The man said they were okay. It appeared no one was injured and no visible damage to the vehicle. It was evident the man was shaken based on his tone of voice.

Finally, we arrived at the hospital. Mama was in the intensive care unit. Uncle Gerald was in the waiting area. He was alone. I could tell from his eyes he had been crying. We hugged me tight when we saw each other. He explained he couldn't call me he didn't know what to say. Mama had severe head trauma was unconscious and on life support. He said, "It's bad, real bad." I went to the nurses' station and advised who I was. Although it was not visiting hours, it was arranged for me to speak with the doctor. The attending physician advised Mama had suffered a severe closed-head injury and blunt-force trauma. Her ankles were shattered. She had a gash across her face which extended several inches. The gash was in close proximity to her left eye. He explained that they placed her on life support because she was not breathing upon arrival to the hospital, and due to no one being present that could make a decision, hospital policy requires they place the patient on life support. The doctor explained that he believed Mama had no brain activity. I asked the prognosis. He explained they could administer a test the following day to determine if there was brain activity. He said if there was no brain activity we would need to decide whether or not she would remain on life support. I asked what the prognosis was if she had no brain activity and remained on life support. He said she would likely be in a vegetative state. Ironically, during Daddy's illness, Robin, Mama, and I had discussed quality of life. Mama told us if something every happened to her and she was in a vegetative state, to not allow her to live. I knew in my heart the decision that would be made should this test confirm no brain activity.

Uncle Gerald went in with me to see Mama. I was overcome. She was physically broken in every aspect. I quietly sobbed, tears streaming down as I rubbed her hand and told her I was there and that I loved her. Her head was bandaged and in a device that stabilized her head and neck. It seemed cords and tube were everywhere. I was unable to stay in her room due to being overcome with emotion. Even though she was unconscious, I did not want to loose my composure in her presence. When I left her room, I cried out hysterically. It was a cry of pain, the type of a cry no parent wants to hear from their child. Shane was in the hall, and he and Uncle Gerald held me up as I was unable to support my own body weight. I cried out, "Why?" Shane and I walked, and we walked for a while to calm me. Once I calmed down, I thought I have to tell Robin. I wanted no one else to tell her.

I felt in that moment, I put the whole armor of God on. "Put on the whole armor of God, that ye may be able to stand against the wiles of the devil" (Ephesians 6:11). I felt I was having an out-of-body experience and was in survival mode, a place that felt all too familiar. I called and confirmed Shane's parents were with Robin. Family begin to arrive from Mississippi and Huntsville. I made sure everyone understood no one was to tell Robin. I would speak with her in person. Later that Christmas Day, two of my Daddy's brothers, Uncle Michael and Uncle Prentiss, and Uncle Prentiss' wife Freddie drove Shane and me to visit Robin.

Road conditions had improved some, but were still rough. I spoke with Robin alone. I explained to her the extent of Mama's injuries. We cried together, both asking "why" and feeling life was not being fair to us. We felt cheated, robbed! I attempted to reassure Robin that we would be okay no matter the outcome. Robin and I agree we would have the test administered the following day to assess for brain activity, and if no brain activity was recorded, we would remove her from life support. Neither of us wanted life support removed today, Christmas Day. This being her favorite holiday, we did not want to associate it with her death in years to come. We agreed that I would return back to Birmingham to be with Mama.

The next day, December 26, was the day. They ran the final evaluation to assess for brain activity. Mama had no brain activity. Robin was stable, and the hospital discharged Robin to allow her to say her goodbyes to Mama. Robin would have a long road to recovery. Due to her injures, she would be in a wheelchair for some time and would need assistance with activities of daily living and rehabilitation. Robin arrived in Birmingham. We were surrounded by family, both maternal and paternal relatives.

Robin and I went and said our goodbyes to Mama. I was still numb from losing Daddy. I now felt numb, empty, and lost. The life support was removed, and she was gone. Robin and I held each other and cried. I had never experienced this type of pain and wanted no one else to experience it. It's an emotional pain of the heart. It's a pain no medication and no words can heal. In that moment, I thought I will never heal from this pain. I remember, in that moment, getting an upsetting phone call. A distant relative phone inquiring about Mama and asked about her physical appearance as he had heard she did not look like herself. I thought I would be unable to contain myself. God guided my tongue in that moment as I refused to comment and abruptly ended the phone conversation. I was shocked and in disbelief that someone could have the audacity to ask such a question during this difficult time.

I called the funeral director in our hometown. I told him who I was and about the death of Mama. After I identified myself and my need, he rhetorically asked, "Didn't we *just* bury your father?" I said, "Yes sir." He said he was in disbelief as he had known my parents for years.

I remembered Mr. Richmond coming to the house when I was a little girl. Mr. Richmond asked if I could give him a moment to collect his thoughts; he said he was in disbelief. There was silence. The phone conversation resumed, and he advised he would make arrangements for a local funeral home in South Alabama to pick up her body. He explained it was state law her body had to be emblemed before crossing state lines. I told him he had approval to do what needed to be done. We agreed that he would notify me once he had her back in Mississippi, and we would discuss a time to visit his funeral home to make arrangements. Mama use to say, "You know where you have been, but you don't know where you're going." So true!

There was a lot of family at the hospital. Robin and I agreed it was best we return to Huntsville tonight and leave for Mississippi tomorrow. Some relatives returned to Huntsville and others returned to Mississippi.

Robin and I were in separate vehicles on the drive to Huntsville due to her limited mobility and wheelchair. I didn't sleep much that night; my thoughts were racing. I was thinking of all that had to be done, and I would primarily be reasonable for getting things done. Robin was in no physical or mental condition to handle the arrangements. Unknowingly, in the moment, I became the "rock." Just as Mama had been the rock of the family, I had to assume that role; it was now just the two of us.

It was Sunday, and we left Huntsville and headed to Mississippi. Shane stayed in Huntsville and would come to Mississippi later for funeral services. We arrived home and settled in as much as possible. The house felt cold and empty.

My parents had built the family home in 1968. Robin and I were both raised in this house and had shared so many memories with Mama, Daddy, family, and friends. My memories immediately following Mama's death are vague. People were coming and going for the next week, visiting, praying with us, bringing food, and offering words of comfort. It felt all too familiar having done this just a little over a year prior. I was in an emotional state of shock and disbelief. I suppressed my feelings.

Suppressing my feelings allowed me the ability to go through the motions of making funeral arrangements and getting things done. On Monday, we were scheduled to make funeral arrangements. Robin was unable to assist in arrangements. She was experiencing complications from her injuries and was taken to the emergency room. Relatives took her to the emergency room; while others supported me at the funeral home. I selected a soft gray casket with a light pink lining. Robin and I had no issues selecting what Mama would wear. There was a new off-white dress hanging in her closet and off white was pretty on her. She wore the off-white dress with an angel pendant. Mama wore an angel pendant every day. The casket spray ordered was full of her favorites, various shades of pink flowers and roses.

After Robin was released from the emergency room, we worked on the obituary. The obituary was prepared, and Mama's favorite poem was inserted in the obituary, *When I Must Leave You* by the Late Helen Steiner Rice. The poem speaks of living after death and not being afraid to die and meeting again "in the sky."

During that week, I clearly remember high-school friends visiting to offer condolences. A friend, Cheryl, I had not seen since high school was among those who visited. Her visit was special as we had known each other since first grade.

I called my employer and spoke with my supervisor, and I advised her of Mama's passing and requested a delay in my start date. She was more than accommodating; she expressed her condolences and advised to contact her at a later time to discuss my start date. She assured me my position would remain vacant until I was able to begin work. Although I had no idea what was ahead of me, I felt a sense of relief knowing I would have income to support myself. I phoned and spoke with my apartment manager and advised I would be delayed in moving to my housing. She was accommodating as well, and just requested I maintain contact with her to ensure she keep a unit available for me.

Saturday arrived one week following Mama's death, and it was time for the funeral. Friends and colleagues of Robin's traveled from North Carolina to support her. Shane, friends, and my sorority sisters traveled from Huntsville. There was no visitation held for Mama. As we prepared and made funeral arrangements following Daddy's passing, Mama let us know her wishes. She wanted services brief, closed casket, no visitation, and burial next to Daddy. Our cousin, Pastor Davis, gave the eulogy for Mama just as he had for Daddy a little over a year prior. I have clearer memories of Mama's services.

During the services, Robin and I intermittently sobbed. I thought to myself, *My final 'lifeline' is gone. How will I go on?* The emotional pain seemed unbearable. I remember during the eulogy, he compared Mama's life to the game of baseball, her favorite sport. Pastor Davis had a close relationship with Mama and Daddy. He and Mama spoke nearly daily until he and his family relocated to Huntsville.

He shared with the congregation that Mama was ready to be with the Lord; she had accomplished what she wanted but most importantly what God wanted her to accomplish in her temporary home. As in baseball, in life, Mama had loaded the bases and was ready to be with the heavenly father. First base was caring for Daddy throughout his illness; second base, was Robin graduating from college, and third base was Daddy suffering no more and going to be with the Lord. My graduating from college was a home run, and she was now at peace.

I believed she was ready as she had struggled since Daddy's death, but I was not ready for her to go. I knew that it was not about my timing but about God's timing. "To everything there is a season, and a time to every purpose under the heaven: A time to be born, and a time to die; a time to plant, and a time to pluck up that which is planted" (Ecclesiastes 3:1).

CHAPTER

6

GRIEF

The reality of my parents being gone was beginning to set in. Family and friends had returned to their respective homes. The comings and goings had lessened at Mama's and Daddy's house. Robin and I had to begin preparing for the next phase of our lives. Robin and I agreed Uncle Gerald would continue to reside in the house. I would temporarily return to Huntsville until I relocated to Birmingham. Robin would reside with Pastor Davis and his family in Huntsville to receive the care and treatment she needed. She would take an extended leave from her job to recover and rehabilitate.

Eventually, Robin and I returned to Huntsville. I continued to avoid processing my grief and loss. I welcomed distractions. Distractions were helpful throughout the day but at night I cried myself to sleep for months. I found my thoughts racing. I still did not clearly understanding how or why Daddy had to die, what "really" caused the multiple myeloma, why did Mama have to die, who did this, why did he flee the scene, were they really investigating the accident, would we every know who hit them, we have to settle Daddy and Mama's affairs, obtain her death certificate, maintain the house, I have to prepare to move, will I like Birmingham, will I like my job, will I be able to support myself, who will love me unconditionally, who will I talk to everyday, who will support me in all I do without judgement? I know God said he would be a father and a mother "when my father and my mother forsake me then the Lord will take me up" (Psalm 27:10). God said when parents leave due to death or abandonment he will take you up as he has always been with you. But I questioned God, he is intangible. Many of these questions haunted me for years to come.

After returning to Huntsville, while on a visit to Robin at the Davis' home, they gave us all the salvageable items from Robin's car. Shane was with me when they presented me and Robin with the items. There were wrapped Christmas gifts from Mama for the three of us. Robin, Shane, and I unwrapped our gifts. Many of the gift boxes were dented from the impact of the car accident. Emotions were mixed. I laughed a little more on this day than I cried. I still felt an emptiness. I missed my Mama. She always had a way of making me feel special. One of my gifts from Mama was an engraved name plate for my desk. In her usual fashion, she was always attentive to detail. This name plate is in my office today. She and Shane had an ongoing conversation about his need for a toaster and his need for house slippers. A toaster and house slippers were among his gifts. Although the gifts may seem insignificant, they were significant in that they were the last gifts we would receive from Mama. I knew she was gone.

The day had come for me to leave Huntsville and move to Birmingham. I had already moved my furnishings and belongings. It was a Sunday and I was to start work on Monday. Pastor Davis could see the pain in my eyes as I struggled to fight back tears. He had us to stand in a circle and hold hands; his wife Dora, Robin, Shane and myself as he prayed for me. I remember him asking God to strengthen me as I took the next step in my life and feeling alone without my safety net. He prayed for removal of my fear and for peace. As he prayed I remember the tears flowed. I felt my strength dissipate. I was physically and emotionally weak, but I had to move forward with the move and the new job.

Over the next months I visited Huntsville most weekends to visit with Shane and Robin. During the week I isolated myself. I only engaged with my coworkers while at work. In the evenings I would get dinner and retreat to my apartment. My weekly out-ing was to the grocery store and gas station. Shane would visit on occasion and I would engage in more activities during his visits. I continued to attend church either in Huntsville or Birmingham. I was feeling increasingly disconnected from God. I withdrew from friends. Eventually I was no longer active in the sorority. I lost interest in things I enjoyed and had no motivation to engage in activities. In my mind my friends didn't understand because they had not lost their parents. Not realizing that parents can be living yet absent. People I knew and didn't know were reaching out with calls and cards. Graduate sorors had learned of my loss and sent cards. Sorors in the local Birmingham Chapter reached out to me as well. I was thankful and appreciative, but my life had been shaken. I wanted to be alone and in limited company. My plans and future no longer seemed realistic. I was disappointed in the world. The world was not "just." Good things happen to good people and bad things happen to bad people. I had lost faith in God and faith in myself.

Robin was regaining her strength and planning to return to work in North Carolina. Shane proposed I said "yes." I left the insurance company and Birmingham and relocated to Decatur, Alabama. I was still consumed with settling Mama's and Daddy's affairs. College graduation commencement was approaching, I was planning a wedding, house hunting and seeking another job. I continued to compartmentalize and distract myself from my emotional pain. May arrived and I participated in the commencement ceremony. I literally went through the motions of commencement. College graduation typically is a joyous time but for me it felt as it was something to check off a bucket list. I remember how proud both Mama and Daddy were when we attended Robin's undergraduate and graduate school graduations. Neither Mama or Daddy liked pictures but on those occasions they both smiled for the cameras. Although family and friends traveled to be with me for graduation I felt empty. It was if I had an open wound that would not close.

Later in the year Shane and I married and purchased a home. I found a job with an insurance agent in the same company I had worked previously. Robin returned to North Carolina. After returning to North Carolina Robin realized she needed and wanted to be closer to family, so she relocated to Georgia. She resided with

Aunt Eva for a while because she was still recovering. Robin and I were both lost and trying to re-establish ourselves and felt the voids. I obtained my insurance license in the State of Alabama at the request of the insurance agent. While working at the insurance agency one of my co-workers encouraged me to write the local news station about the accident. Months had passed. It was approaching a year since Mama had died, and the case had been closed. Based on my last contact with the investigator, he advised they had a strong lead. The lead subsequently fell through. I was suspicious based on the fact that the investigator was extremely confident in the lead, identifying the person to me and their background. Due to the investigator's description of the person and their professional background, I questioned if he were found responsible for the accident, whether or not he would be held accountable. I wrote a letter to a local newspaper and an investigative reporter contacted me to do a story about the hit-and-run accident. It was nearly Christmas when he interviewed me, and the story was aired. Robin and I offered a reward, but the driver was never located. Today, the hit-and-run driver has not been identified.

I had given up on a career in social work. Social work no longer seemed possible. I had lost my passion and desire to help others and to impact the world as I had hoped. I was angry and still lost, thinking who is helping me. Where are the people that visited and called? Where are those people asking those two famous questions: "How are you doing" and "Do you need anything or call if you need something?" Where was God? I felt a sense of loneliness and hopelessness for the future. No one was reaching out to help fill that void. My parents had been so many things to so many people, now their children were left motherless and fatherless. My reoccurring thought was *"How do I go on?"* Yes, you put one foot in front of the other, but that's hard to do when you feel you're not going anywhere. There is a difference between where I was psychologically and where I was physically.

I resigned myself to a career in insurance. After years of experience in the insurance industry, it was something familiar. I had become extremely knowledgeable in homeowners and auto insurance. But insurance was not my passion. I felt what I wanted and needed was no longer important. I wanted Mama and Daddy to live and they didn't. Nothing else "really" mattered. Eventually, I received an opportunity to be an insurance agent selling insurance for several insurance companies. I would primarily sell auto and homeowners and some life insurance. I took the opportunity. While continuing to work in insurance I decided to attend graduate school, studying for a Master of Science degree in Organizational Leadership. My plan was that a graduate degree would allow for more career opportunities; most importantly, it was a distraction. Several years had passed since Daddy and Mama's deaths. I continued to struggle to find happiness. Most people would have assumed I was happy as I was on my way to the American dream. The reality is that things and people did not complete or fulfill me.

Shane and I attended church regularly. Each Sunday, after church, we would have dinner with his dad, stepmom, siblings, and niece and nephew. They were a blended family. Shane's dad had three children, and his stepmom had two children. I enjoyed the family dinners and gatherings. Often, the dinners would consist of other church members and their families. Everyone should sit around, laughing and talking. But I felt no inner peace. I felt disconnected from God. My relationship with God reminded me of a relationship with a distant relative. You know them, but you don't know them— you see them at weddings and funerals, you only call for special occasions.

I would often look through the many cards I had received from Mama over the years and the cards received from friends and family following her and Daddy's deaths. I would sob as I thought of the many memories of Mama and Daddy. I remember one day as I was looking through the cards I found a letter I had written to Mama while in college letting her know what she and Daddy meant to me and how thankful I was to have them as my parents. As I continued to look I stumbled on one of Mama's favorite poems *"Miss me but let me go"* by Edgar Albert Guest. The poem speaks of the love individuals share and letting your loved one go but remembering the love by acknowledging the journey of life. In that moment I had an epiphany, realization that I must live life. I knew Daddy and Mama would want me to live life and live on in their memory. "The Lord is nigh unto them that are of a broken heart; and saveth such as be of a contrite spirit" (Psalm 34:18).

7

FORGIVENESS

Continuing to long for peace and happiness in most aspects of my life, I decided to apply for a position with a child welfare agency. It was months without a response from my application. I was not surprised as I still felt hopeless and lacked faith. Finally, I was contacted for an interview. I interviewed for a position as a case manager for family and children services. Subsequently, I was contacted and offered the position; which I accepted. After a few days of shadowing coworkers I felt the job was a natural fit. The work environment was positive and there was a genuine desire from staff and supervision to ensure the safety and welfare of children. After about a year I was past my learning curve and had become increasingly confident in my skills and abilities and knowledgeable of child welfare policies and procedures. I was responsible for making recommendations to supervision and the courts that could potentially change the lives of families and children. This was a responsibility to not be taken lightly. I made a concerted effort to treat all families and children with dignity and respect, being driven by policy and to only impose my professional judgment in decision making. For the first time in years I was regaining faith in myself and finding happiness in my profession. As I learned more about case management and social work I was motivated to know more.

I was still working on my graduate degree. I began to question whether or not I should continue to pursue this degree as I was unsure if I would be able to use this degree if I were to continue to pursue a career in social services. Realizing my follow though these days was lacking I decided to follow through with completing my degree. I was not raised to be a quitter. Over the years I had found myself leaving tasks and goals incomplete.

A year later and three days before the fourth anniversary of Mama's death our first child was born, a daughter. She was almost a Christmas baby. I was thankful and overjoyed to have a beautiful daughter. Shane stayed home with me for the first six weeks to help and bond with the baby. After twelve weeks I returned to work and completed my graduate degree four months later. Our routine of Sunday dinners had not changed. My in-laws had grown with more marriages and more children. My relationship with God seemed unchanged. I continued to give him reverence but my connection with him remained lost. Things begin to shift when I was called into a meeting at work with a member of leadership. During the meeting I was strongly encouraged to obtain my graduate degree in social work. My administrator advised of my potential growth in the field of social work; explaining to me to advance in the field a graduate degree was required. I listened attentively yet thinking to myself there was no way I could purse another graduate degree with work, being a wife and a mother. He recommended I read a book that he had read and found helpful to him in many aspects of his life. *Purpose Driven Life by Rick Warren.* I expressed my appreciation to my administrator advising I would consider his recommendations. I obtained a copy of the recommended book and began reading. The book held my attention as I felt it was written specifically for me. It challenged me to begin to challenge my thoughts and thought process. I begin reflecting over the past several years of my life. Realizing that self-evaluation was required for my personal and professional growth I began a self-evaluation.

Through my evaluation I realized that anger was controlling my life. I was angry at God for allowing things to happen to my parents that caused their deaths and angry that no one was held accountable for their deaths. Because I lacked control of my life and had no power to change the tragic experiences anger manifested itself in me. I allowed my anger to become internal which had become self-destructive to me. My anger had me in bondage. "Be not hasty in thy spirit to be angry; for anger resteth in the bosom of fools" (Ecclesiastes 7:9). Anger drove my unwillingness to forgive. How could I forgive the man that hit and killed Mama and injured Robin. He failed to own what he had done; assumed no responsibility. Just as my anger my lack of forgiveness held me in bondage. Through self-evaluation I recognized that I had lost relationships and connections with friends and loved ones. Most importantly I had drifted from God.

Once my sole lifeline, cheerleader, spiritual guide, best friend was gone I was left with the lessons, values, and beliefs I had learned in my twenty-two years of life. I was unable to use those as positives to assist in my coping due to being consumed with anger and an unwillingness to forgive. Anger and the unwillingness to forgive gave me a false sense of power and control. Many people believe if they don't forgive someone, the person that wronged them has lost a relationship, a friend, a source of financial or emotional support. The lack of forgiveness more often than not has little to no impact on the person that wronged but more of an impact on the person that has been wronged. Even though I had drifted from God I knew that God had power, but I questioned the limits of his power. I was raised to believe that God had all power he was Jehovah Jireh the Lord will provide, Jehovah Rapha the Lord that heals, Jehovah Nissi the Lord is my refuge, Jehovah Shalom the Lord is peace. If he had all "this" power, why did the things in my life happen? I began to pray but my prayers were not the same as they had been. I did not ask God for understanding and clarity as to why Mama and Daddy died but for discernment. Discernment being the process of thinking biblically; thinking in truth and refuting false teachings. In 1 Thessalonians 5:21–22 God instructs Christians to use discernment "prove all things; hold fast that which is good. Abstain from all appearance of evil. Folly is joy to him that is destitute of wisdom: but a man of understanding walketh up rightly" (Proverbs 15:21). "Who is wise, and he shall understand these things? Prudent, and he shall know them? For the ways of the Lord are right, and the just shall walk in them: but the transgressors shall fall therein" (Hosea 14:9).

As I began to slowly reconnect with God and understand his word, I prayed about my future and his plans for me. Working in child welfare restored my desire to help others. I told God my desire was to be a change agent in the lives of others. I wanted to be in a profession and a position that I could show others love, provide support and encouragement, give them hope, and restore their faith in humanity. Psalms speaks of David and his belief and trust in God "Delight thyself also in the Lord; and he shall give thee the desires of thine heart" (Psalm 37:4). During this time, I continued working with families and children and had been promoted to supervision. God used work situations to show me hypocrisy in others, so that I could recognize my own hypocrisy. How could I provide all the things to others and encouraged others to not be angry and forgive when I myself was angry and withholding forgiveness for my fellow man. I questioned myself asking how can you justify your anger and inability to forgive when God is a forgiving God. He was crucified, hung, and nailed to the cross but "Then said Jesus, Father forgive them; for they know not what they do, And they parted his raiment, and cast lots. And the people stood beholding. And the rulers also with them derided him, saying, He saved others; let him save him-self, if he be Christ, the chosen of God. And the soldiers also mocked him, coming to him, and offering him vinegar. And saying, If thou be the king of the Jews, save thy self" (Luke 23:34–36). How am I above God and not willing to forgive when God is a forgiving God he forgave those that ridiculed him. I asked for discernment and was given discernment. God was not responsible for Daddy and Mama's deaths. "For God so loved the world, that he gave his only begotten Son, that whosoever believe the in him should not perish, but have everlasting life" (John 3:16). God gave people "free will" to make choices. When people make choices they may make the choice to sin. Satan's goal is to destroy that which is good and he uses people to destroy that which is good. God created all things to glorify him. God created Adam and Eve knowing they would sin. If we never sin we never know grace. He tests us here in this world to prepare us for eternal life with him. Everything that I was enduring or will endure God had already endured. The man that hit and killed Mama and injured Robin had volition to be responsible for his actions but chose not to. "It is not for me to seek vengeance withholding forgiveness, It is God that avengeth me, and subdue the people under me" (Psalm 18:47). Dearly beloved, avenge not yourselves, but rather give place unto wrath: for it is written, VENGEANCE IS MINE, I WILL REPAY, saith the Lord" (Romans 12:19). I was beginning to understand Mama's unwavering faith.

It was clear to me that if I wanted to grow spiritually, professionally and personally I had to forgive. "For if ye forgive men their trespasses, your heavenly Father will also forgive you: But if ye forgive not men their trespasses, neither will your Father forgive your trespasses" (Matthew 6:14–15). Sin is sin, no sin is bigger or smaller. Just as the man was responsible for the accident that changed my life, sinned I had also sinned. Romans 3:23–24 "For all have sinned, and come short of the glory of God; Being justified freely by his grace through the redemption that is in Christ Jesus." I forgave him and prayed he sought forgiveness for his actions. I felt a sense of peace in my heart and spirit. I knew God was pleased as I continued to make efforts to be closer to him.

8

HOPE

I had become increasingly comfortable working in social services. I developed relationships with community providers, law enforcement and the judicial system. In order to maximize my potential in the field it was imperative I obtain my graduate degree in social work. I applied and was accepted to graduate school, subsequently I was accepted to the graduate social work program. Through my graduate studies I obtained the skills and knowledge to be an effective social worker and social work administrator. I developed an understanding of psychosocial development, social work theories, racial and ethnic relationships, direct social work practice and an understanding of human behavior. While studying I learned more about myself and my thought processes. In order for me to effectively advocate for others, help others problem solve, cope, and improve their social functioning and overall well-being I had to become more self-aware of any personal bias, issues or concerns that would affect my ability to serve others. Graduate school help restore hope in myself and society. To be amongst others with like minds and the goal to serve others was encouraging.

While in graduate school I was presented with issues that would affect completing my degree but each time I doubted myself or the process God reminded me of his grace and mercy. God extends his grace and mercy to us because Jesus his son died for our sins and gave us salvation as "the gift of God." We receive grace through faith.

Even when I experienced doubt I had faith God's will would be done. During graduate school I had to complete two field placements. I was concerned as to how I would complete my field placements and work full-time. The agency in which I was employed had an educational leave program which would allow me to work part-time while continuing to receive full-time pay. I would have to sign a contract agreement that I would continue to work for the agency for two years following completion of my degree. I applied and was accepted into the program. I became ill the summer I was to begin my first field placement with a rare condition called erythema nodosum. Erythema nodosum is a condition of the skin. The skin becomes inflamed primarily on the sheens and legs. Painful red nodules form and resemble bruises. Often the nodules have fever and cause difficulty in walking due to swelling. Recovery from erythema nodosum is typically three to six weeks unless chronic. Its linked to a number of conditions including strep throat, fungal diseases, and sarcoidosis. Erythema nodosum is also linked to medications. I was sent to specialist to determine the cause in hopes of preventing the illness in the future. I was able to continue with classes and my field placement even during my illness. I connected with a graduate social worker that own a social service agency that was willing to supervise my first field placement. She was understanding of my limitations due to my medical condition and allowed me to work around my limitations to complete my field placement hours. By the end of my field placement I had recovered from erythema nodosum. It took approximately six to eight weeks for me to completely recover. As I placed more faith and trust in God he continuously gave me grace and mercy.

My second field placement would be more extensive then the first it would be a two-semester field placement within a single agency. I hoped to obtain a field placement with the social service agency in which I was employed in a neighboring county. Initially I was told the agency was selective in the colleges and universities in which they were accepting field placement students from and they were reluctant to accept me for a field placement with their agency. I was confident that this was the agency in which I was to complete my field placement for several reasons; I would be able to obtain knowledge and experience in other areas of social services specifically quality assurance, foster parent and day care licensing. With experience in various areas of social services I would be more marketable in the future. My prayers were no longer for my will to be done but for God's will to be done. I prayed and I believed his will would be done. How could I follow someone I did not trust. I was learning to follow God was to trust God. A licensed graduate social work administrator within the agency I was seeking placement advised she was willing to supervise me for two semesters. I was extremely grateful for her willingness to supervise me. It was my mission to change the view of the agency in hopes they would be willing to supervise other field placement students in the future from my university. By the completion of my field placement I had connected with a number of staff as well as volunteer members of their quality assurance team. They were impressed by my hard work and knowledge of the various programs within the agency. I had completed my coursework requirements; including field placement and was prepared to take my comprehensive exam. I took and past my comprehensive exam and was preparing for graduation. The graduate program was a two-year program. I was blessed to complete the program in a year and a half. My sister, niece, aunt and uncle from Mississippi came to celebrate my graduation. Although I was overjoyed I had accomplished a goal set ten years prior it saddened me that Mama and Daddy were not physically present for my third college graduation. Commencement exercises were held outside. As I obtained my degree I looked to the skies knowing they were there in spirit. I had no idea and still have no idea what the future holds but I have a redefined definition of hope.

Hope is a feeling and belief that one can have what is wanted or desired. When one is a believer hope with God is certain. Romans 5:2–5, "By whom also we have access by faith into his grace wherein we stand, and rejoice in hope of the Glory of God. And not only so, but we glory in tribulations also: knowing that tribulation worketh patience; And patience, experience and experience hope: And hope maketh not ashamed; because the love of God is shed abroad in our hearts by the Holy Ghost which is given unto us." Hope can be misplaced when someone is a nonbeliever or a believer experiencing trials or tribulations. We must remember when our hope is anchored in Jesus Christ and not other people or material possessions our hope is solid because hope gives us faith. Because "now faith is the substance of things hoped for, the evidence of things not seen. For by it the elders obtained a good report. Through faith we understand that the worlds framed by the word of God, so that things which are seen were not made of things which do appear" (Hebrews 11:1–3). "But without faith it is impossible to please him: for he that cometh to God must believe that he is, and that he is a rewarder of them that diligently seek him" (Hebrews 11:6).

9

FAITH

After graduation I returned to work full-time. I felt more equipped to serve. My skills and knowledge in the field of social work had increased. I was able to more effectively lead my staff to perpetuate the principles and values of social work as they worked to serve families and children. Often times public servants are ill equipped to serve; failing to be self-aware of the impact of personal values and beliefs on those they serve and transferring personal experiences to others. Becoming a licensed professional social worker assisted in ensuring the "integrity of the profession and protecting the public." I was beginning to see how my spiritual growth was beginning to align with God's plan for my life.

Once I obtained my license as a graduate social worker and completed my obligation to the agency. I began to question was it God's plan for me to continue to serve in this role. For over eight years my work had focused on families and children. Recognizing the needs of the community were not limited to families and children, I prayed diligently for guidance. In Psalm 32:8 "I will instruct thee and teach thee in the way which thou shalt go: I will guide thee with mine eye." I begin to explore other opportunities for growth. Those close to me questioned me considering leaving a position of leadership for a position with less status. People are often impressed by status and titles but earthly status and titles have no place in defining who we are with God. I was proud of my position, the services I had provided, my role within the agency and the relationships I had developed within and outside the agency and community. Sometimes in life to move forward you have to take steps perceived as backwards to others but forward to ourselves. You must "look with your spiritual eyes and not be physically blinded." I had interviewed and was offered a position and was unsure about accepting the position. I had been in salary negotiations and was awaiting a response. One day while in my office I prayed quietly to myself immediately, after I finished praying I received a call they had accepted my offer. This was confirmation of his plan. The time had come to say goodbye to the agency. There were so many things I loved about the agency and my job. I loved my co-workers and serving families and children. To be able to assist in the safety and welfare of God's children was a blessing. I was able to reunify families and children, witness children obtain a forever family through adoption, assist children with learning to live independently, share with children their losses and successes. In my professional career this was the hardest job to leave but I knew it was his will.

Over the next several years I worked with various communities and populations providing social work case management services. As a social work case manager I was responsible for completing psycho-social assessments to assist in identifying clients and family's needs and assisting with accessing services to meet identified needs. In order to effectively help clients and families I used the person-in-environment approach, assessing each component of the individual and family systems to determine the effects of each component on the whole system. Social work case management is coordinating a wide array of services to meet the individual and family needs including but not limited too; housing, employment, substance abuse treatment, child care and mental health services. The goal is to provide clients and families with resources and services to improve their lives. The ultimate goal is to improve society. One of my greatest struggles as a social worker was encountering individuals and families residing in unsafe, unsanitary, and uninhabitable living conditions. I wondered why God allowed some individuals to be less fortunate than others, why were individuals exposed to abuse and neglect. In the field of social work I was exposed to situations and circumstance they were beyond comprehension and often "why" was never ending.

I found it hard to be a believer and say, "I don't know or I don't have an answer," but the truth is even those that are believers living for God don't know and don't understand all things. I do know that God said we would have pain and suffering, he speaks of pain and suffering in John 16:33 "These things I have spoken onto you, that in me ye might have peace. In the world ye shall have tribulation but be of good cheer; I have overcome the world." Being a child of God, servant, and professional social worker, it was and is my job to intervene and provide compassion and empathy while networking with agencies and the community to uplift others.

Looking back over my life I understand how and why I lost hope and faith in God and questioned God and his power. Even though I accepted Christ as my personal Savior at the age of twelve I was not in a relationship with God. Just as in any relationship, for the relationship to grow you must nurture that relationship, spend time with the person. You must get to know their likes and dislikes, their values, their beliefs, their family. I knew God by way of my parents but was not in a relationship with God. I had not spent time with God getting to know him by studying his word. When my parents died I was not equipped to logically process the losses, so I learned defense mechanisms to help me cope. Defense mechanisms help keep unwanted feelings and people away. The use of defense mechanisms can be unconscious, they can make the individual feel better.

I was in denial, I isolated myself and suppressed my feelings. Over time my use of defense mechanisms led to complicated grief. Complicated grief resembles depression. Complicated grief can result from the sudden loss of a loved one, a loss from a car accident or disaster. It can manifest itself differently in individuals. I experienced extreme emotional pain when I thought of my loved ones, I felt numb, I lost purpose, I lost trust in people and was unable to enjoy life. Complicated grief can lead to post traumatic stress disorder based on circumstances surrounding the loss.

Individuals grieve expected losses differently than traumatic, sudden or unexpected losses. When a loss is expected the individual is able to emotionally and psychologically prepare to some degree. A traumatic loss can be devastating it changes the world as the individual has known it. The individual can be left feeling lost and vulnerable. With traumatic or sudden losses the loss is more complicated with circumstances surrounding the loss.

When an individual is in a relationship with God hope builds faith and faith builds trust. These three combined equips an individual to overcome any loss or situation they encounter. Non-believers most often look internal to self or external to others to help them grieve the loss of a loved one or assist with issues and concerns that may arise. Believers and nonbelievers both experience pain, believers seek comfort and strength from God because of their faith and trust in God. The Bible tells us there will be tests and trials. If we are planted in his truth we will be able to stand the trials and test of life. Our faith is refined when we experience trials "that your faith should not stand in the wisdom of men, but in the power of God" (1 Corinthians 2:5). "That the trial of your faith, being much more precious than of gold that perisheth, though it be tried with fire, might be found unto praise and honor and glory at the appearing of Jesus Christ" (1 Peter 1:7).

10

TRUST

Trust is something that most people value in a relationship with someone else. It allows someone the ability to believe in the character and integrity of someone. Most often when trust is extended it is extended completely. When we have trust in an individual we believe that individual will be a source of support and encouragement in good and bad times. I felt I was in a good place spiritually and emotionally. Shane and I were expecting our second child. We waited to the end of the first trimester to share the news with our daughter. The day after we told our daughter she would be having a brother or sister, I received a phone call from the nurse advising the doctor was concerned from the ultrasound that fetal growth was inconsistent with my anticipated due date. My lab results had been reviewed and the doctor wanted me to complete additional labs the following morning. The labs showed my human chorionic gonadotropin hCG levels were dropping. In a normal pregnancy the hCG level should increase doubling every two to three days. It had been a day since I saw the doctor had an ultrasound and labs. The nurse explained it could be a sign of impending miscarriage but it was not definitive. I felt a sense of numbness, I was emotionless as I was processing the news. I begin to pray I asked for strength. I knew that he knows all my needs and will supply them. The Philippians met Paul's needs and because of their sacrifice God meet their needs "But my God shall supply all your need according to his riches in glory by Christ

Jesus" (Philippians 4:19). I discussed the phone call with Shane later that evening. Neither of us was rash in our thoughts, we agreed I would have the labs completed as scheduled. We were hopeful there was another explanation for the doctor's concerns other than miscarriage. The following day I presented to the hospital alone. Shane was working. They completed another ultrasound and drew labs. It seemed as if it took hours for them to return as the doctor wanted to review the ultrasound and lab results prior to discharge. During this time my thoughts were racing, what is happening in my body, did I do something wrong, how will I tell my daughter, will I be able to have more children. Later that afternoon the nurse and doctor came in and advised I was impending miscarriage. The options were explained to me "miscarry naturally or a D&C." As she explained the physical process of a natural miscarriage and a surgical procedure dilation and curettage, it became a blur. Things were running together. I was told to explore my options and contact my doctor's office in the morning. Both expressed their sympathy. After they left I cried silently tears rolling down my face. I called Shane and shared the news I could feel his empathy.

That evening I shared with our daughter we were not having a baby. We cried together and hugged one another. It was a relief she asked few questions. She seemed to accept the news as I explained to her we had to trust God. I was hurt and confused but knew this would be a process for something greater to come. Shane and I discussed the options. I shared concerns related to miscarriage and my body. He was supportive and understanding in that I had to make the choice I felt most comfortable. Two days later I had a dilation and curettage. Shane was with me for the procedure. I was nervous about being under anesthesia. The nurse and anesthesiologist spoke with me prior to me drifting off to sleep. I was in recovery for approximately an hour prior to discharge. They gave me something light to eat and drink since I had not eaten or drank since the previous day. Shane tried to lighten the mood with his corny since of humor. Following the procedure we headed home the mood was somber conversation was minimal. I was empty, a life I was to give birth to was gone. It seemed something had been taken from me. Another loss! Could I handle another loss my parents, my grandparents, a child. Why did this happen to me. My first pregnancy was ideal no complications. When I began to question and doubt the process Satan tried to use this as an opportunity to draw me from God. Satan often comes in a disguise through individuals. He uses individuals to fill in the gaps during your weakest and most vulnerable moments. I refuted Satan just as Paul told us to stand in Ephesians 6:10–12 "Finally, my brethren, be strong in the Lord and in the power of his might. Put on the whole armor of God, that ye may be able to stand against the wiles of the devil. For we wrestle not against flesh and blood but against principalities, against powers, against the rulers of the darkness of this world, against spiritual wickedness in high places." In order to stand and refute Satan I trusted God believing that the emotional and physical pain I was experiencing was required in order for me to be blessed. A few days after the dilation and curettage I had a follow up appointment. I was examined by my physician and she advised I was healthy. I was physically able to conceive and carry a child to term. I was relieved.

In life it often feels as if we have one challenge or one problem after another. Six months after the miscarriage I had an unexplained lesion on my foot. I was seen by a dermatologist he recommended a biopsy due to the concern of melanoma. He recommended the biopsy be performed same day in his office. The biopsy was performed and I was advised I would be contacted in a couple of days with the results. I was not shaken by the concern for melanoma. I knew that God was on my side and whatever the outcome he was with me. When you trust him completely you allow him to bear your burdens. "Casting all your care upon him: for he careth for you. Be sober, be vigilant; because your adversary the devil, as a roaring lion, walketh about, seeking whom he may devour" (1 Peter 5:7–8). The lesion was noncancerous. The dermatologist recommend referral to a surgeon to remove the lesion explaining that the lesion could become cancerous. He explained if melanoma is left untreated unlike other cancers it will spread rapidly. I was seen by a surgeon within two days of the referral. The surgeon agreed the lesion needed to be removed due to an increased risk of melanoma if the lesion remained.

The physician explained risk involved. He advised the foot was an extremity that is known to heal slower than other parts the body. I remained unshaken, I continued to have faith in God and his healing. There was no hesitation I requested the surgery be scheduled. I was scheduled for surgery the following week. Although I was concerned and nervous being put under anesthesia I trusted that God would work through the nurses, anesthesiologist, and surgeon that all would be well without any complications. My sister came and was with me for the surgery and a couple days after to provide support and assistance. There were no complications during or following surgery. I was able to return to work within a few days and my foot was completely healed in a couple of weeks. Exodus 15 speaks of God being a healer Jehovah Rapha he is "the healer of all diseases, I am the Lord that health thee."

Often trust is misplaced into self or others. When you are in a relationship with God you are obedient to him, placing all trust in him and not self. In God he will work through you to be a blessing to others and work through others to bless you. Adam and Eve were disobedient to God trusting self. God told Adam "And the Lord God commanded the man, saying, of every tree of the garden thou Mayest freely eat. But of the tree of knowledge of good and evil, thou shalt not eat of it: for in the day that thou eatest thereof thou shalt surely die" (Genesis 2:16–17). In the word of God there are three deaths physical death, spiritual death and eternal death. God then made Eve so man would not be alone. The serpent spoke and questioned "yea, hath God said, ye shall not eat of very tree of the garden and the woman said unto the serpent, we may eat of the fruit of the trees of the garden: But of the fruit of the tree which is in the midst of the garden God hath said Ye shall not eat of it neither shall ye touch it, lest ye die" (Genesis 3:1–3). The serpent came which was Satan "sin" in disguise and told them the tree was a good source of food so they ate. God made the world good and perfect "And God saw everything that he had made, and, behold, it was very good. And the evening and the morning were the sixth day" (Genesis 1:31).

Evilness came from man and not God. When God made Adam and Eve he gave them free will. The ability to make choices. Some individuals will make good choices and others will make bad choices. Two people can be given the same opportunity but based on their individual choices their outcomes may be different. Individuals want to blame God when something bad or undesirable happens. Is God the blame? God is not the blame and holds the individual accountable for their choices. Why does he not intervene and exercise his power when someone sins? If God intervened would you learn right from wrong? God parents us just as children should be parented. God knows and sees all. Unlike God, parents don't know and see all but have life experiences that allow them to see things their children are unable to see. Parents aren't always able to shield and protect their children from pain and suffering. There are potential joys, pains, and heartaches of parenting but do they prevent people from having children? Should God prevent people from pain and suffering? Throughout Daddy's illness and following his death Mama attempted to protect and shield Robin and me from pain and suffering. Because she had experienced the illness and loss of her mother she knew the emotional pain we would experience. She was unable to shield us from our grief and loss. I had to endure pain and suffering. We all have to go through a process and learn for ourselves. In that process we will experience pain and suffering. It is during those times that our relationship with God should sustain us. In Luke 1:17, the word speaks of children having to endure in order to be "prepared for the Lord. And he shall go before him in the spirit and power of Elias, to turn the hearts of the fathers to the children, and the disobedient to the wisdom of the just; to make ready a people prepared for the Lord."

When we are obedient to God his blessings are abundant. A month following the foot surgery we learned we were expecting. The ultrasound indicated the baby was healthy, and growth was consistent with the anticipated due date. Three months later we learned it was a boy. I believe I was more excited than Shane that it was a boy. Once learning the sex of the baby, I began to the think of the many stories I had been told about the relationship of a mother and son. When Jesus is on the cross being crucified he expresses his love and concern for his mother as she was grieving "When Jesus therefore saw his mother and the disciples standing by, whom he loved, he saith unto his mother, Woman, behold thy son. Then saith to the disciple, Behold thy mother: And from that hour that disciple took her into his own home" (John 19:26–27). A mother's love for her child and a child's love for their mother is everlasting love. Even on the cross Jesus wanted to protect his mother from his pain and suffering.

During my second pregnancy I continued to work in social work, I was the program manager for a social service agency. By this time, I had been in the field for ten years and had worked with various populations and in a number of positions. I was unsure of my future in the field but had plans to continue my social work career. I was contacted by a colleague that had over twenty-five years' experience in the field, she advised of a job opportunity for a national organization that served veterans. The organization was seeking a social work case manager to provide direct practice to homeless veterans. As she shared the specifics of the position, I thought of my relatives that had served or were serving in the armed forces. I specifically thought of one of my favorite uncles, Uncle Chuck. Uncle Chuck was a man of immense strength and courage not only because of his military service but because of his gentle and kind spirit for his family and others. He had served a number of deployments in his nearly twenty-five years of service including Vietnam and Korea. I explained to my colleague I was expecting and felt unsure of a career change at this time. She encouraged me to consider the position, reminding me pregnancy was a temporary condition and positions as this were rare and could be career changing. I told her I would be prayerful and allow God to lead me. Galatians 5 speaks of walking in the spirit of God and not in the flesh. If we are to live a life pleasing to our heavenly father we are to be led by the spirit "this I say then, walk in the Spirit, and ye shall not fulfill the lust of the flesh" (Galatians 5:16). I applied for the position and subsequently was offered the position months later. I didn't understand why God wanted me to give up my current position in what I felt was a time of great uncertainty in my life. It is hard to give up complacency but God spoke in Mark 10:21, "Then Jesus beholding him loved him, and said unto him, One thing thou lacks: go thy way, sell whatsoever thou hast and give to the poor and thou shalt have treasure in heaven: and come, take up the cross, and follow me." I trusted and followed God. At seven months pregnant I gave up my position and accepted a new position.

CHAPTER

11

ACCEPTANCE

I was thirty-eight weeks pregnant and had been in my new position approximately six weeks, when I began experiencing excessive swelling. I spoke with the nurse and she advised if swelling had not decreased over night to present to the hospital in the morning for testing and an evaluation by recommendation of the doctor. I presented to the hospital prior to work with thoughts I would present to work following my evaluation. It was my last scheduled work day prior to maternity leave. After initial blood work and testing I was advised I would be placed on bed rest for the reminder of my pregnancy. Additional test results indicated my platelet count was dropping. My blood pressure was elevated, and I had experienced a rapid weight gain due to increased fluid. All symptoms were consistent with preeclampsia. Preeclampsia is a condition where a woman experiences high blood pressure, high levels of protein in the urine and often swollen feet, legs and hands. Women that develop this condition have stable blood pressure prior to pregnancy. To treat the condition the baby must be delivered otherwise the symptoms will worsen causing eclampsia to develop; which can be fatal. Within minutes I went from bed rest to the baby would need to be delivered today. The physician explained the baby was not in distress, but I would begin receiving medications to assist with inducing my labor. The only cure for preeclampsia was to deliver the baby. She advised it would likely be hours before the baby would be delivered. I would be unable to have an epidural due to the low platelet count and would have to give birth naturally or by cesarean section. Through this process I remained calm. I began to make phone calls as I was not prepared for delivery that day. I called Shane and he began to make arrangements to leave work and come to the hospital. Shane arrived to the hospital several hours later. As my labor progressed and contractions became more frequent and more intense I began to experience fear. My thoughts began to race thinking of all the horrific stories I had been told about natural child birth. Satan waits and responds like a leech, ready to leech on to irrational thinking causing one to doubt their faith. Before Satan had an opportunity I began to pray asking God for an uncomplicated delivery and a healthy baby. I knew with childbirth there would be pain and God designed woman to be able to endure the pain of childbirth. It would be a temporary physical pain that would bring immense joy. John 16:21 speaks of the anguish experienced during childbirth "A women when she is in travail hath sorrow, because her hour is come: but as soon as she is delivered of the child she remembereth no more the anguish for joy that a man is born into the world." Nine hours after arriving to the hospital I had an uncomplicated delivery and gave birth to a healthy baby boy.

It is human nature for our faith to be questioned when we encounter and unfamiliar situation especially those that involve physical and emotional pain. Even though the word of God speaks of pain and suffering and that they are essential for spiritual growth we continuously question why must we experience pain and suffering. Instead of questioning "why" the pain and suffering, remember it is preparing us for God's purpose and plan for our lives. In James 1:2–4, it tells us we are to count all trials and tribulations with great joy. When we realized God has given us victory over trials and tribulations we spiritually mature. Often we want the blessing of God without the sacrifice. God made the ultimate sacrifice when he gave his only son. Jesus Christ died he was placed in a tomb, was buried and rose from the dead for us to have eternal life. "For God so love the world, that he gave his only begotten Son, that whosoever believeth in him should not perish, but have everlasting life" (John 3:16). His death on the cross was payment for our sins; his sacrifice gives us complete forgiveness. Scripture tells us "for all have sinned, and come short of the glory of God" (Romans 3:23).

Acceptance is the act of accepting or receiving someone or something as it is offered. Jesus Christ accepts all of his people as they are and offers them salvation without cost. Because of free will individuals have the choice whether or not they accept salvation. Salvation is the saving of the soul. In Genesis 4:6–7, God in love gives Cain and opportunity to right his wrong. He tells Cain the consequence of his choices. He told him sin would abound in him if they did not sacrifice from the heart. In an outburst of anger Cain kills his brother and with arrogance, Cain disrespects God when he ask of Abel's whereabouts. "And the Lord said unto Cain, Where is Abel thy brother? And he said, I know not: Am I my brother's keeper? And he said, What hast thou done? The voice of thy brother's blood crieth unto me from the ground. And now art thou cursed from the earth, which hath opened her mouth to receive thy brother's blood from thy hand: When thou tillest the ground, it shall not henceforth yield unto thee her strength; a fugitive and a vagabond shalt thou be in the earth. And Cain said unto the Lord, My punishment is greater than I can bear" (Genesis 4:9–13). Cain had the volition to do right or wrong, he chose wrong and this is what began violence among our fellow man; which is the direct result of Adam and Eve sinning.

We are cleansed through salvation. Once someone accepts Jesus Christ as their personal Savior the process begins, developing an intimate relationship with our heavenly father. Living a Godly life requires one to order their steps in the word of God. To be about the purpose and plan God has for our lives we must evolve holistically in the following areas spiritually, personally and professionally. As we evolve in these three areas we will be able to effectively work in our purpose while following God's plan for our life. If we fail to evolve holistically God cannot and will not use us for his purpose and plan. Individuals may define spirituality differently; most define spirituality as connecting with a higher being someone or something that is abstract. Spirituality may be demonstrated through organized religion; prayer; meditation. In biblical terms spirituality means "being spiritually minded which is to dwell in the Holy Spirit to be controlled by the Holy Spirit." When we are controlled by the Holy Spirit and not the flesh we are pleasing to God "so then they that are in the flesh cannot please God" (Romans 8:8). After returning to work from maternity leave I was increasingly focused on pleasing God allowing the Holy Spirit to dwell in me. Often we are selective in inviting God to be Lord of our life we don't allow him to completely reside within us. We treat God like a house guest while visiting you can only occupy certain rooms. When he dwells in us he lives in us he is occupying us completely. Once I allowed God to dwell in me I began to see his call on my life. I was working in my calling and had been for ten years and was spiritually blinded and unable to see his purpose and plan for my life. One is spiritually blinded when we are guiding ourselves not allowing our faith in God to lead us. What is visible to the natural man differs from what is visible to the spiritual man. In 1 Corinthians 2:14–15, "But the natural man receiveth not the things of the Spirit of God: for thy are foolishness unto him: neither can he know them because they are spiritually discerned. But he that is spiritual judgeth that all things yet, he himself is judged of no man." For years I was looking with my physical eyes and was spiritually blinded. When we began to see with our spiritual eyes we spiritually mature. Spiritual maturity leads to personal maturity and personal maturity leads to professional maturity.

Personally individuals are often focused on self and their individual needs. They are typically oblivious or unconcerned about others unless it's of their benefit. Individuals are more willing to associate and give to someone that can give something in return. As an individual spiritually matures the Holy Spirit moves within their heart and radiates like the sun into other aspects of their life. The individual begins to remove people, things, and habits from their life in order to walk in his purpose. To follow God you may have to give up an unhealthy relationship, financial wealth, status, or material possessions. "We have to remove all things that block our access to God." Following God is to be a servant humbling ourselves, so God does not have to humble us. In Mark 10:17–21, it tells of the young ruler "And when he was gone forth into the way, there came one running, and kneeled to him, and asked him, Good Master, what shall I do that I may inherit eternal life? And Jesus said unto him, Why callest thou me good? There is none good but one, that is, God. Thou knowest the commandments, Do not commit adultery, Do not kill, Do not steal, Do not bear false witness, Defraud not, Honour thy father and mother. And he answered and said unto him, Master, all these have observed from my youth. Then Jesus beholding him love him, and said unto him, One thing thou lackest go thy way, sell whatsoever thou hast, and give to the poor, and thou shalt have treasure in heaven; and come; take up the cross, and follow me." When I got out of my way God was able to work through me. Nemesis differ for individuals. My nemesis was power and control. I wanted all power and control of my life personally and professionally. I had a plan for my life and had not consulted God about my plan and God humbled me. After losing my parents I was broken and blinded. No one but God had the ability to move me from my brokenness and blindness. My emotions had blocked my access to God. But God humbled me. I had to give up who I was to receive God's blessings. Our family often helps define who we are and once my parents died the intact family unit was gone, the core of who I was, was no more. I was in my early twenties young, naive, and living by the guidance and direction of my parents. Because the closeness with extended family and friends gradually faded after the loss of my parents, I had to solely depend on God.

Through my spiritual and personal maturity, God placed me in a professional position to continue his purpose and plan for my life. Working with the homeless was one of the most humbling experiences of my life. No one knows what their fellow man or woman is experiencing unless they voluntarily share. Often we fail to understand the complexity or magnitude of one's situation or circumstance. As a social worker providing case management services to the homeless, I not only had an opportunity to assist my patients with obtaining and maintaining housing, I got to know them personally. To effectively advocate for my patients I had to engage them to thoroughly assess them. I learned about their childhood, family, personal and professional relationships. I learned about their underlying issues that may have been a contributing factor to their homelessness; which may have included but was not limited to substance abuse, mental health, and unemployment. Often judgement is past based on the appearance of a person and not their character. Many of my clients had lost their dignity and self-respect. The community often shun them treating them as if they were worthless and inhumane. To assist my clients with obtaining and maintaining housing I was responsible for transporting them on housing searches and other appointments within the community. I was often saddened by the stares, glares, abrupt tones of voice and disingenuous behaviors of others towards my clients. God allowed me to be the vessel to be a voice for others, to assist with restoration of dignity and respect by demonstrating God's love to others through kindness and compassion. John spoke of love being one of God's many attributes "Beloved, let us love one another: for love is of God; and every one that loveth is born of God, and knoweth God. He that loveth not knoweth not God; for God is love" (1 John 4:7–8). The four years I worked in this position I saw some lives remain the same and others change. I saw God's love and the power of healing; clients maintaining housing, obtaining employment, recovering from addiction, and obtaining self-sufficiency.

Once we remove everything from us that is not like God we are able to live for him. Everything that we do should be to glorify God. The life we live is not for self but for God and others. When we are selfless we live to be a servant. In 1 Peter 5:6 it tells us "humble yourselves therefore under the mighty hand of God, that he may exalt you in due time." Once the Holy Spirit dwells within you personally it can dwell professionally. I was hungry for God and to continue to do his will. I wanted to be professionally equipped with the knowledge needed to continue my professional growth. I became a licensed independent clinical social worker (LICSW). Subsequently I obtained my private independent practice license (PIP) in case management and clinical social work. This would increase opportunities in the field of social work to serve others. I was nervous about transitioning from case management to clinical social work. Over time we become complacent. I had become complacent in my job and was fearful of the unknown. Even though I had fourteen years of experience, numerous credentials, I questioned my knowledge, skills and abilities to work as a clinical social worker. I felt I needed more years of experience, so I avoided seeking positions in clinical social work. I resorted back to that old thinking of my plan not God's plan. Just as nonbelievers, Christians can loose focus and turn from God and listen to self. The holy spirit began moving in me reminding me to be obedient and trust God just as God charged Joshua "Have not I commanded thee? Be strong and of a good courage; be not afraid, neither be thou dismayed; for the Lord thy God is with thee whithersoever thou goest" (Joshua 1:9). After four years I literally stepped out on faith and transitioned from case management to clinical social work.

I was beyond nervous to begin a new chapter in my life. For years I told myself I would "never" work in mental health. I felt I had nothing to offer. How am I qualified to treat someone with depression, anxiety, post-traumatic stress disorder, schizophrenia, bi-polar disorder, or any other diagnosis? How would I effectively provide psychotherapy to someone that may be grieving the loss of a loved one, divorce, retirement, or manage general life stressors? What will I say? What treatment modality will I use? Will the patients engage with me? Will I do more harm than good? I struggled with the role and responsibilities of being a clinical therapist. This was a defining moment for me. I would have to develop a different style of engagement. I prayed. I was humble. I asked God to remove me and work through me, guide my thoughts, guide my tongue "The Lord God hath given me the tongue of the learned, that I should know how to speak; a work in season to him that is weary; he wakeneth morning by morning, he wakeneth mine ear to hear as the learned. The Lord God hath opened mine ear, and I was not rebellious neither turned away back" (Isaiah 50:4–5). I told God I was unsure why he had trusted me to serve in this manner, but I trusted him and knew this was his will. The more one comes to know Jesus Christ the more he lives within. The individual becomes selfless knowing that they should be solely working to glorify God.

As I settled into my new position I realized the hand of God was on me as I had not experienced before. It felt surreal! God used me in ways I did not realize I could be used. I found myself overwhelmed with emotion when I reflected on how God worked through me to be a blessing to someone. One may ask, How do you know its God? I know its God because he guides my thoughts. I may think I have no words, God gives me words. I may feel tired or weak but God lifts me up to lift someone else up. I listen to the verbal communication of my clients and witness their nonverbal communication. I see and feel their emotions. The client returns and has applied behavioral changes or used techniques or skills discussed in session, symptoms have lessened, barriers are no longer barriers, stressors have been reduced or minimized, suicidal ideations have lessened. This is what trusting God will do. I understand why God chose me for this purpose. He chose me because I submitted myself unto him putting all hope, faith and trust in my heavenly father. When we take off all that is not of God we are a new creation in Christ. "And that ye put on the new man, which after God is created in righteousness and true holiness" (Ephesians 4:24). God wants us to be relatable to one another. He wants us to have and demonstrate agape love, biblical love. "Beloved, let us love one another: for love is of God; and every one that loveth is born of God, and knoweth God" (John 4:7). We all were created different and unique in God's image but we are all equal. Often we are divided by race, ethnicity, religion or socioeconomic status but in God we are one. In God's call for my life those things that create division have no place. People are hurting spiritually, emotionally and physically and are in need of encouragement and support that comes from someone that is sincere in God's purpose and not blinded by things of the world.

12

RESTORATION

It had been over fifteen years since losing my parents and I have complete clarity of why I lost them when I lost them. God had to break me to bless me. He could not use me as I was he had to tear me down to build me up to use me for his purpose and plan. I was in my early twenties the next chapter of my life was to be written. In the first chapter of my life my parents were there providing the nurturing and guidance I needed. God will humble us, test our faith and test our trust in him "And he humbled thee, and suffered thee to hunger, and fed thee with manna, which thou knewest not, neither did thy fathers know; that he might make thee know that man doth not live by bread only, but by every word that proceedeth out of the mouth of the Lord doth man live" (Deuteronomy 8:3). God wants our hearts to be pure and true to him. He wants to know our true motivation for following him, God tested the children of Israel. In John 6:47–50, "Verily, verily, I say unto you, He that believeth on me hath everlasting life. I am that bread of life. Your fathers did eat manna in the wilderness, and are dead. This is the bread which cometh down from heaven, that a man may eat thereof, and not die. I am the living bread which came down from heaven; if any man eat of this bread, he shall live forever; and the bread that I will give is my flesh, which I will give for the life of the world." Manna is the "bread of heaven." It is what God provided as he led the children of Israel the Israelites to the Red Sea. God knew they would be in the wilderness for forty days without food thus providing the manna. Manna resembles a coriander seed and taste of wafers with honey. The word of God says the manna can only be harvested on certain days and in a limited quantity only enough for them to eat that day "Then said the Lord unto Moses, Behold, I will rain bread from heaven for you; and the people shall go out and gather in a certain rate every day, that I may prove them, whether they will walk in my law, or no. And it shall come to pass, that on the sixth day they shall prepare that which they bring in; and it shall be twice as much as they gather daily" (Exodus 16:4–5). The manna was not provided on the Sabbath and if the manna was not preserved as ordered by God it would become wormy and could not be eaten. Because the children of Israel lived by their faith and trust in God, when Joshua and the children of Israel crossed over the Jordan they entered the Promise Land and the manna ceased because in the Promise Land they would eat the produce to supply their physical needs.

God provides just what we need when we need it in the exact quantity that we need. Routinely we associate someone's growth and development with their age. There are various theories of human growth and development and stages of psychosocial development. These are all relevant. They assist clinicians in assessing individuals, making recommendations and providing services. But spiritual growth and development does not always correlate with behavioral and cognitive psychology theories. Being in my early twenties I was a young adult, college graduate, ready to enter the work force and establish my independence. According to Erikson's stages of psychosocial development I was in stage six, "intimacy versus isolation." In this stage it's important that close relationships are developed, if you're successful at this stage you're likely to form long term relationship that are secure. Each stage of development builds on the previous stage, so I had to have mastered stage five, "personal identity versus confusion." Personal identify is knowing who you are; which is shaped by interactions and experiences. Our identity "guides our actions, beliefs, and behaviors as we age."

I am reminded of a message entitled "I am under construction." Construction can be used as an analogy for life. When your building something you typically build in phases and must go in a designated order to obtain completion, just as it is indicated in stages of human growth and development, cognitive and psychosocial develop. I did not realize I was under construction, spiritual construction. My parents were my "manna." They were here for a season and purpose they had provided what I needed. They laid a strong physical solid foundation. Just as God speaks in the book of Luke 6:48–49, "He is like a man which built a house, and digged deep, and laid the foundation on a rock; and when the flood arose, the stream beat vehemently upon that house, and could not shake it: for it was founded upon a rock. But he that heareth, and doeth not, is like a man that without a foundation build a house upon the earth; against which the stream did beat vehemently, and immediately it fell; and the ruin of that house was great." It was now time for me to live by faith and trust in God to complete construction. In the midst of my grief I was unable to see his purpose or plan for my life. My anger and my unwillingness to forgive impaired my thought process. I felt no one was helping me. I was losing my desire to help others. I realized perceptions and expectations of helping and supporting others rest in the eye of the beholder. With only a foundation he had to begin construction and build me up. Eventually the walls were up with a roof the covering, doors the barriers and windows the spiritual lenses. Once the exterior is in place he can began work on the interior. God was working on the inner me and continues to work on the inner me. Once the dwelling is complete there is always maintenance. As I live the remaining chapters of my life, I live solely for God and will continue maintenance to maintain his dwelling. I accept and embrace what I have been through, I accept and embrace all imperfections as all have shaped me into who I am today. When we accept Jesus Chris as our personal Savior man does not move us "But none of these things move me, neither count I my life dear unto myself, so that I might finish my course with joy, and the ministry, which I have received the Lord Jesus, to testify the gospel of the grace of God" (Acts 20:24).

Once we accept Jesus Christ as our personal Savior his grace and mercy allows for a "do over or reconstruction." Life is hard, and God knows the enemy will strike in any manner to draw you to him and away from God. When you find yourself withdrawing from God, lost, defeated, hopeless, helpless be reminded he is a forgiving God, he is a God of second chances. Before you sin, God knows of your sin. He is concerned with how you respond when you fall short of God's glory. Individuals often react versus respond. Reacting is an impulsive response unlike responding is a thought process. Do you react or respond? Do you impulsively give up and return to the world or do you respond and continue to follow God? It's easier to be of the world than to follow God. Following God requires sacrifice. It may require ending unhealthy relationships and changing behaviors. Because your human God knows you may be tempted to return to those unhealthy relationship or behaviors. It's easier to be of the world then of God. The rules of the world can be changed to fit your needs but in God the rules remain the same for all his children. In his word it tells us that God does not change he remains the same "today, tomorrow, and forever."

Even in your mess God is still with you "for by grace are ye saved through faith: and that not of yourselves it is the gift of God. Not of works, lest any man should boast. For we are his workmanship, created in Christ Jesus unto good works, which God hath before ordained that we should walk in them" (Ephesians 2:8–10). It's his grace and mercy that allows for a "do over, reconstruction, or restoration." What is required of Christians is straightforward but its blocked by things of the world and the flesh lacking self-control. In Acts 3:19–21, Peter teaches a sermon on repentance and the forgiveness promised by God "repent ye therefore, and be converted, that your sins may be blotted out, when the times of refreshing shall come from the presence of the Lord; and he shall send Jesus Christ, which before was preached unto you: whom the heaven must receive until the times of restitution of all things, which God hath spoken by the mouth of all his holy prophets since the world began."

The obstacles you encounter are positioning you for a blessing from God. Life is like a relay race. In the race you must be in the right position to receive the baton, in life you must be in the right position to receive your blessing. You will never receive the baton unless you're in the right position and the race is not finished until the baton has been past to all members of the team. In God people want to claim victory without the work. The victory in any spiritual race is not about being swift but enduring to the end as written in Matthew 24:13, "but he that shall endure unto the end, the same shall be saved. I returned, and saw under the sun, that the race is not to the swift, nor the battle to the strong, neither yet bread to the wise, nor yet riches to men of understanding, nor yet favour to men of skill; but time and chance happeneth to them all" (Ecclesiastes 9:11).

13

DESTINATION

When you're going through life and face adversities individuals fail to see "problems as possibilities" for opportunities. Embracing possibilities for opportunities leads to your destination. No one knows their destination, today, tomorrow or forever. It's important to prepare to secure your destination. When you're in covenant with Jesus Christ he will position you for today, tomorrow and for eternity. The destination for a believer is eternal life with the heavenly father. It was years before I realized that each obstacle prepared me for the next obstacle; which is preparation for my ultimate destination. As I overcame obstacles and adversities I became spiritually stronger. As you grow spiritually the obstacles and challenges you face will become more complex. In school your promoted to the next grade based on passing and mastering the courses required for your current grade. With each grade level the expectations increase as your knowledge increases. God will test your faithfulness. He cannot spiritually evaluate you until your faithful over a few things. The Lord spoke in the parables of the talent saying, "His Lord said unto him, well done, thou good and faithful servant: thou hast been faithful servant; thou hast been faithful over a few things, I will make thee ruler over many things: enter thou into the joy of thy Lord" (Matthew 25:21).

The simplicity of God is made complex by the disobedience of flesh. If you're aspiring for something greater than what you have or where you are in life, you must be diligent in the present to have greatness tomorrow. Why would God give you a better job with better pay, better benefits, increased responsibilities and more opportunities for growth, if you fail to be faithful in a job that requires less? The story of David is the essence of faithfulness. Samuel was an aging prophet and the people of Israel wanted Samuel to appoint a king. Samuel was reluctant and did not want to appoint a king, because the people insisted Saul became king. Saul was thirty years old when he became king and reigned as king for forty-two years. Years past and Saul was misusing his position as king which caused worry to Samuel. Samuel warned Saul that God would remove him as king if he did not follow God. Saul chose to boldly disobey God twice. God told Samuel worry not he would appoint a new king in time. (1 Samuel 13:13–14), Saul would be king no more. He commanded Samuel "fill a horn with oil" and to go to Bethlehem of Judah and find Jesse, he had chosen one of Jesse's sons to be king. Samuel was concerned about going because he did not want Saul to know a new king had been appointed, fearing Saul would kill him. God instructed Samuel to take a cow as an offering to the Lord and invite Jesse and his sons to the sacrifice. This would distract the people from God's ultimate plan. Jesse's sons came to the sacrifice and God initially did not identify any of them to Samuel as king. He told Samuel to ask if there were any other sons and Jesse said he had one remaining son of his eight sons; his youngest son fifteen-year-old David. David means "beloved" in Hebrew. David was in the field tending to his sheep. The Lord commanded Samuel to pour oil on David which was anointing him to be king. The people thought David was being anointed to be a prophet as Samuel. From that day forward David followed the Spirit of God and began to show his greatness. David returned to his duties as a sheep herder after being anointed. Meanwhile David continued to practice throwing his sling of stones, so he could kill any animal in the wild that posed a risk to his sheep. Because of his accuracy he could strike and kill with one swing of his sling. Although David was young in years, but he was spiritually mature. David had a relationship with God and they spoke with each other frequently. He was a young man who was "a man after God's own heart" (1 Samuel 13:14; Acts 13:22).

Saul became distraught after God stopped speaking to him. The voice of the Lord left Saul because of his disobedience. Just as God stopped talking to Saul he will stop talking to any of his children to remind his children that he is God and "obedience is better than sacrifice." Saul now had difficulty controlling his emotions, on occasion he was overcome by evil spirits. "But the spirit of the Lord departed from Saul, and an evil spirit from the Lord troubled him" (1 Samuel 26:14). The sound of the harp would calm Saul when he became upset and was unable to control his emotions, so he called for Jesse to send his son David to play the harp and sing for him. While David was with Saul, Saul had David carry his armor; his shield, spear, and sword. God was placing David in position to receive the ultimate blessing. Being given this responsibility was preparation for the next opportunity. Later David went on to fight Goliath. Everyone was afraid to stand against Goliath, but David was not afraid. He was not intimated by Goliath's large statue he knew he was equipped with a plan and what was required to defeat Goliath. There had been an ongoing conflict with the Philistines. Three of David's older brothers were in the army and went with Saul to battle the Philistines. Jesse his father sent David to his brothers with "parched corn, ten loaves and ten cheeses." Before Jesse left he prepared for a sheep keeper to watch over his sheep. David was faithful in his job as a sheep herder, he realized after he played the harp for King Saul that God had greater works for him. David exemplifies obedience and faithfulness. He continued to labor on God's behalf unknown of God's purpose and plan for his life. When you work to please God, your focus is spiritual maturity not worldly positions or possessions.

David arrived at his brothers and heard of Goliath's challenge. The men of Israel fled from Goliath in fear. "And David spake to the men that stood by him, saying, what shall be done to the man that killeth this Philistine, and taketh away the reproach from Israel? For who is this Philistine, that he should defy the armies of the living God" (1 Samuel 17:26)? David went to Saul and volunteered to fight Goliath. David told Saul of his experiences as a servant keeping his father's sheep and how the Lord delivered and protected him as he fought a lion and bear "David said moreover, the Lord that delivered me out of the paw of the lion, and out of the paw of the bear, he will deliver me out of the hand of this Philistine, and Saul said unto David, go and the Lord be with thee" (1 Samuel 17:37). Saul becomes jealous of David after he kills Goliath. He realizes the Lord is with David and seeks to kill David. David has slain more than Saul but even though Saul sought to take David's life, David continues his obedience and faithfulness "And David behaved himself wisely in all his ways; and the Lord was with him, wherefore when Saul saw that he behaved himself very wisely, he was afraid of him. But all Israel and Judah loved David, because he went out and came in before them" (1 Samuel 18:14–15).

Being in covenant with the Lord provides protection it shields you from the principalities of the world. With salvation God promises us his covenant for eternity. If you follow David's example you will be guided to "life more abundantly." In John 10:10 God tells us "the thief cometh not, but for to steal, and to kill and to destroy." God places a covering over David "Incline your ear, and come unto me: hear, and your soul shall live; and I will make an everlasting covenant with you, even sure mercies of David" (Isaiah 55:3). Saul attempted to surround people around David that would work on his behalf to kill David. He arranged for his daughter Michal to marry David and for his son Jonathan to befriend David, "And Saul spake to Jonathan his son, and to all his servants that they should kill David. But Jonathan Saul's son delighted much in David: and Jonathan told David, saying, Saul my father seeketh to kill thee: now therefore, I pray thee, take heed to thyself until the morning, and abide in a secret place, and hide thyself: And I will go out and stand beside my father in the field where thou art, and I will commune with my father of thee; and what I see, that I will tell thee" (1 Samuel 19:1–3). Most think the greatest loyalty is with family and there is no relationship greater than that of a biological blood relationship. In God the greatest loyalty is to him, his purpose and his plan. When you're in Christ "blood is thicker than blood." Christian are united by the blood of Christ. In a spiritual union nothing and no one can "separate you from the love of God." Because David had God's covering Saul was unable to kill or have David killed. Even Saul's son turned from his father's request of wrong doing to protect David. Jonathan defended David against Saul "And Jonathan spake good of David unto Saul his father, and said unto him, Let not the king sin against his servant, against David; because he hath not sinned against thee, and because his works have been to thee-ward very good: [5] For he did put his life in his hand, and slew the Philistine, and the Lord wrought a great salvation for all Israel: thou sawest it, and didst rejoice: wherefore then wilt thou sin against innocent blood, to slay David without a cause" (1 Samuel 19:4–5)? When you shed all that is not of God and give your heart and soul to God he will place people among you to love and support you as you walk out your Christian journey to seek his kingdom. These are the people that pray with you and pray for you when you are unable to pray for yourself. These are the people that give you love unconditionally. These are the people that give you unsolicited truth. You must use discernment in relationships and rid yourself of relationships that are not of God. "Be ye not unequally yoked together with unbelievers: for what fellowship hath righteousness with unrighteousness? And what communion hath light with darkness? And what concord hath Christ with Belial? Or what part hath he that believeth with an infidel? And what agreement hath the temple of God with idols? For ye are the temple of the living God; as God hath said, I will dwell in them, and walk in them; and I will be their God, and they shall, be my people. Wherefore come out, from among them, and be ye separate, saith the Lord, and touch not the unclean thing; and I will receive you, And will be a father unto you, and ye shall be my sons and daughters, said the Lord almighty" (2 Corinthians 6:14–18).

Over the course of years Saul sought after David and as David flee from place to place he developed a following of people and Saul was displeased. David was able to seek refuge in Moab for his family. He was repeatedly able to escape Saul but "Saul sought him every day, but God delivered him not to his hand" (1 Samuel 23:14). While David was in the wilderness Saul continued to seek David "And Jonathan Saul's son arose, and went to David into the woods, and strengthened his hand in God" (1 Samuel 23:16). The two renewed their covenant before God. God repeatedly created possibilities for opportunities with David. David spared Saul's life at least twice. He continued to trust God and his plan. After the deaths of Saul and Jonathan, David was appointed king nearly fifteen years after he was anointed to be king of Judah. The story of David is a testament to God's grace and mercy when your obedient and faithful. "He that is faithfully in that which is least is faithful also in much; and he that is unjust in the least is unjust also in much" (Luke 16:10).

What is your destination? Are you prepared for your destination? Will your life's works be a reflection of God's plan and purpose for your life? It is clear in the word of God he has a purpose and plan for all of his children. However, we choose whether or not we live in his purpose and plan. The things you do and the life you live are a reflection of who your following. Are you following God or are you following flesh? God provides certainty while the flesh leads to sin; which is disobedience to God. In Joshua 23:14, Joshua challenges the people to trust in God and his word "And, behold, this day I am going the way of all the earth: and ye know in all your hearts and in all your souls, that not one thing hath failed of all the good things which the Lord your God spake concerning you; all are come to pass unto you, and not one thing hath failed thereof." Even when it may feel as if God has failed you God has never failed you. When God does not respond as we feel he should or when he should our irrational thoughts allow us to believe that he has failed us. Most individuals think and feel their thoughts are rational and the way in which they perceive things, people, and situations are the way they are. More often than not, all individuals experience irrational thinking on occasion. Irrational thinking is when thoughts are not based on reason even though there is information to support something to the contrary of what one may think. Intelligence is disregarded in rational and irrational thinking because irrational thoughts "clutter the minds of all people." Irrational thoughts are often derived from defense mechanisms. Defense mechanisms are what we use to cope in life to protect ourselves from people and situations. Defense mechanism may be even use to keep you from a relationship with God. They are often used unconsciously to avoid "unpleasant thoughts, feelings and behaviors". Defense mechanisms present themselves in various forms including but not limited to denial, suppression, fear, compartmentalization, and dissociation.

Believers and nonbelievers limit their spiritual growth through the flesh and defense mechanisms. Unlike the word of God, the flesh provides superficial comfort. The flesh allows people to remain in the world, it rationalizes thoughts, feelings and behaviors that are not of God. When people are in the world they associate themselves with others that are of the world to continue engaging in worldly activities. People want to "be associated with God but no close to God." Being associated with God is like being in an uncommitted relationship. Often individuals want the benefits of a relationship without the commitment. In the book of Galatians 6:5–8, it says, "For every man shall bear his own burden. Let him that is taught in the word communicate unto him that teaches he in all good things. Be not deceived; God is not mocked; for whatsoever a man soweth, that shall he also reap. For he that soweth to his flesh shall of the flesh reap corruption; he that soweth in the Spirit shall of the Spirit reap life everlasting." The most obvious reasons people are kept from the blessings of God is "hurts, habits, and hang ups" God is a God of unconditional comfort, love, grace, mercy, and patience. He wants to free you from all that is not of God your "hurts, habits, hang ups" which have manifested themselves in your life in the form of depression, anxiety, anger, fear, unforgiveness, blame, guilty, or hate." God said if you give it all to him he will bless and "ye might be filled with all the fullness of God. Now unto him that is able to do exceeding abundantly above all that we ask or think, according to the power that worketh in us" (Ephesians 3:19–20). Until you allow God into your heart you will remain in bondage; your spiritual growth will remain limited and flesh will continue to be weak. Your problems, issues and circumstances will continue to consume your life and you will be unable to achieve your destination. Paul speaks of when man joins with our Lord and Savior Jesus Christ "therefore if any man be in Christ, he is a new creature; old things are passed away; behold, all things are become new. And all things are of God, who hath reconciled us to himself by Jesus Christ, and hath given to us the ministry of reconciliation" (2 Corinthians 5:17-18).

References

Baker, J., and Warren, R. (2009). Life's Healing Choices. Rancho Santa Margarita, CA: Saddleback Resources.

Chernoff, Marc. (2017, September 29). 10 Irrational Thoughts Rational People Often Think. Retrieved from http://www.marcandangel.com/2007/06/10-irrational-thoughts-that-people-often-think/

Davis, C. P. (2017, June 30). Multiple Myeloma. Retrieved from http://www.medicinenet.com/ultiple myeloma/page5.htm

Grohol, J. M. (2017, September 13). 15 Common Defense Mechanisms. Retrieved from http://psychcentral.com/lib/15-common-defense-mechanisms

Multiple Myeloma. (2017, June 30). Retrieved from http://www.mayoclinic.org/diseases-conditions/multiple-myeloma/diagnosis-treatment

Multiple Myeloma. (2017, June 30). Retrieved from http://www.webmd.com/cancer/

Multiple-myeloma-symptoms-causes-treatment

Multiple Myeloma. (2017, July 1). Retrieved from http://cancer.net/cancer-types/multiple-myeloma/diagnosis

Preeclampsia and Eclampsia. (2017, October 18). Retrieved from http://www.webmd.com/baby/guide/preeclampsia-eclampsia#1

Pietrangelo, A., and Cirino E. (2017, September 19). Outlook for People with Multiple Myeloma. Retrieved from http://health-line.com/health/cancer/multiple-myeloma-outlook#overview1

The King James Study Bible (1998). Nashville, TN: Thomas Nelson Publishers.

ABOUT THE AUTHOR

Ashley Magee Madry was born and raised in Gulfport, Mississippi. She grew up in a small rural community known as "Side Camp." She graduated from the University Alabama Huntsville in 1998 with a Bachelor of Arts degree in sociology, and in 2001, Ashley graduated with a Master's of Science degree in Organizational Leadership from Southern Christian University. Eventually, she followed her passion to become a professional social worker and begin pursing a Master's of Social Work degree in 2006. In 2008 Ashley graduated with her MSW from Alabama Agricultural and Mechanical University. She has worked in the field of social work for over 16 years, and is a Licensed Independent Clinical Social Worker, certified for independent practice in social casework and clinic social work. Currently, Ashley works as a clinical therapist. Ashley has been married for 18 years; she and her husband have two children, a daughter, and a son.

CPSIA information can be obtained
at www.ICGtesting.com
Printed in the USA
FFHW020156251118
49536652-53917FF